THE EVOLUTION OF MAN

Ann Arbor
Science
Library

THE EVOLUTION OF MAN

by G. H. R. von Koenigswald

Revised Edition

ANN ARBOR

THE UNIVERSITY OF MICHIGAN PRESS

Contents

I.   THE EVOLUTION OF MAN   1

     Geological Time   4

     The Differentiation of Vertebrates   9

     *Family Trees: Eohippus into Horse and
     Moeritherium into Elephant*   14

II. THE PRIMATES   24

     Human Evolution   31

III. FOSSIL ANTHROPOID APES   45

     The Australopithecus Discoveries   63

     The Homo Habilis Discoveries   76

     The Homo Erectus Discoveries   78

     *Neanderthal Man and the Origins of
     Homo Sapiens*   105

IV. TOWARD MAN   126

     The Development of Culture   142

     INDEX   153

I. THE EVOLUTION OF MAN

Until well into the eighteenth century, man thought that the earth was as it had always been—that man, plant, and animal had not changed since the Creation. Modern geology and paleontology (the study of ancient forms of life) have revolutionized our ideas of the past. We now know that the earth was once very different both in appearance and in climate. Many mountain ranges used to be expanses of open sea, and there were once deserts in the heart of Central Europe and tropical plants and animals in the Far North. Geologists have dug up many hitherto unknown forms of life. The life forms grow stranger as the geological layers (strata) from which they are unearthed grow older. These ancient forms of life often appear in one stratum but not in the next; at the same time, we cannot simply assume that they died out, for many of the species that appear in the later strata belong to the same genus as those that have disappeared. Only the theory of evolution can give a satisfactory explanation of the link between these different but related forms of life. As more fossils are found, geologists are constantly narrowing the gap between animals of successive strata.

Through the ages, parts of the earth have been repeatedly flooded, and periods of sudden geological change have alternated with periods of gradual erosion. As a result, no continuous stratum was ever laid down over any part of the earth. Instead, we find the strata broken by movements in the earth's crust, or intermingled because deposits were not carried to the sea at a constant rate. These apparent breaks in individual strata have misled past observers, and Cuvier in particular, into speaking of a "universal deluge." Cuvier's theory has since been generally rejected.

None of the mammals we know existed before the Ice Age. If we go back further, to the Cretaceous Period, the only mammals we find are pouched animals (marsupials) and insect-eaters. The oldest and most primitive mammals are found in the Upper Triassic horizon (c. 180,000,000 years ago). Earlier Triassic strata, especially in South Africa, reveal only those mammal-like reptiles (now extinct) from which all mammals were derived. If we go back further still, there is no sign of such reptiles—the only vertebrates are amphibians. Below this level, fishes represent the most highly evolved forms. Hence there was a clear development from fish to amphibian, from amphibian to reptile, and finally from reptile to mammal. The evolution of mammals can only be explained as part of the evolution of the vertebrates.

Mammals are not alone in having reptilian ancestors: *Archaeopteryx*, found in the topmost Jurassic stratum of Southern Germany, is classified as a bird because of its feathers. However, it had a distinctly reptilian skeleton, with teeth, a long tail, and claws on its wings. *Archaeopteryx* represents the halfway stage between reptile and bird.

Man himself is a late product of evolution. Modern research has shown that his history cannot possibly go as far back as many have thought. Just as mammals gradually evolved from nonmammalian forms, so man originated from nonhuman forms.

Two hundred years ago, when Linnaeus set up his *Systema Naturae*, he believed that there were as many species then as there had been at the Creation. His zoological approach was as static as the philosophy of his day. Later, when earlier forms of life were discovered and the problem of the relationship between apparently different groups of animals was posed, it became imperative to introduce a chronological system of classification. Linnaeus was the first to recognize that man did not hold the unique place in nature on which he prided himself. He proved that man was simply one of many members of a larger order, which he called Primates because they took first place in his system. Man himself was fitted into the genus *Homo* and the species *sapiens*—thinking man. The genus *Homo* contained another species, *Homo troglodytes*—the chimpanzee. Apparently, this classification did not worry either Linnaeus' contemporaries or his precursors since, in the Middle Ages, the chimpanzee was considered to be a pygmy—a human dwarf. Though Linnaeus was therefore the first to have raised the question of man's relationship to the apes, which was so hotly contested in Darwin's time, he ignored the question of man's descent.

Great differences between man and the anthropoid (manlike) apes are often overlooked by primitive races. Those who know Malayan will tell you that the name of the great Indonesian anthropoid ape, the orangutan, means "man of the woods."

When Darwin published his *On the Origin of Species* in 1859, paleontology was still in its infancy, and the general public knew almost nothing about its findings. The book created a sensation and sold out on the day it was published. While Darwin took care to say nothing about man as such, it was obvious that his remarks applied to our species as well.

Two great zoologists of the time applied Darwin's work explicitly to man. In 1863, Thomas Huxley wrote his *Zoological Evidences as to Man's Place in Nature,* which discussed the problem of man's descent and showed that, anatomically, man was closer to the anthropoid apes than the latter were to monkeys. In 1868, Ernst Haeckel continued this work in Germany. He delivered a great many popular lectures in which he succeeded in rousing the interest of the general public. Nowadays it is difficult to imagine how much of a stir these new ideas created at the time, and what repercussions they had on nineteenth century thought as a whole. This interest gradually waned, largely because of the lack of the kind of spectacular corroboration that paleontologists later produced. For a long time paleontology remained a stepdaughter among the sciences, for it was not until after 1925 that it was able to present a series of fundamental discoveries concerning man's prehistory. We tend to forget that primate fossils are extremely rare. Most primates are arboreal animals, whose remains, even if they are spared by carnivores, are corroded by the acid humus of the forest soil.

Clearly, the problem of man's evolution could only be solved by the results of comparative anatomy, physiology, embryology, zoology, and paleontology, and not by bold theories. The pieces of the great puzzle were put together only when man was studied in the light of all these disciplines.

In what follows we shall discuss what contribution paleontology has made to the study of man's evolution and what knowledge paleontology has given us 100 years after the publication of Darwin's famous book.

Geological Time

Life is a dynamic process. Had our environment remained unchanged from its very inception, we should, of course, have no need to take the time factor into account.

In 1654 it was still possible for Archbishop Ussher of Ireland to state that the world was created at 9 A.M. on October 26, 4004 B.C. Geologists, by discovering vast systems of geological strata, showed conclusively that the earth and life on it must be very much older than that.

We do not propose to discuss the details of all the methods that have been used to calculate geological time, for most of them are now of purely historical interest. It was once believed that the age of the earth could be inferred from the total thickness of all geological strata taken together. Later, the answer was thought to lie in the total salt content of all the oceans, which rough calculations gave as 16,000,000,000,000,000 tons. As it was believed that annual salt deposits amounted to 158,000,000 tons, a simple calculation showed that the oceans must be at least 100,000,000 years old.

The subsequent discovery that individual strata could be dated by means of radioactive disintegrations introduced far more reliable methods into geological research. Uranium breaks down into one part lead and eight parts helium, while liberating heat. Its complete disintegration takes 7,600,000,000 years. At various times, radioactive minerals have crystallized out of molten terrestrial material to start disintegrating at once. Fluid magma has often penetrated into, and solidified inside, systems of strata of known total age. In all such cases, specific mineralogical changes show clearly that the deeper rocks, resulting from this process, are of more recent origin than the superior strata—though normally the opposite holds true—and the minimum age of the lower layer can be assessed. By comparing cross sections of various strata they can be dated individually.

We now know that the earliest rocks in South Africa are about 2,640,000,000 years old and that the beginning of the Cambrian, when the earliest stratum with a distinct fossilized fauna was laid down, goes back some 550,000,000 years.

It was in the Cambrian then, that the curtain first rose on what we know of the drama of life. However, the pre-Cambrian, from which few fossils are known, must also have been of great importance in the history of life, since Cambrian fossils already include all existing families of invertebrates.

From radioactive disintegrations, we know that before the Cambrian there were at least two major periods of rock sedimentation, the Laurentian, which occurred about 1,100,000,000 years ago, and the Algonkian, which is some 800,000,000 years old. Mighty mountains rose up and disappeared again through erosion before the Cambrian sea flooded the land.

Limestone and slate, granite, and fine sandstone have been deposited at all times. Hence it is by their fossil content that sedimentary rocks must be distinguished from one another and dated. Thus, we use life, or the development of life, as a relative measure of time. Species which were short-lived but widespread serve us as fixed points. These belong to a host of groups—crustaceans, coelenterates, brachiopods, ammonites (a group of extinct cephalopods), reptiles, or mammals.

The names and divisions of successive geological strata have been fixed by international convention, and all countries nowadays use the same colors to distinguish individual formations on geological maps.

Geologists like to divide geological time into historical periods. They speak of ancient (Paleozoic), medieval (Mesozoic), and modern (Cenozoic) geological eras. These eras do not represent anything like identical intervals; in fact, each of them is only about half as long as its predecessor. Incidentally, the older a stratum the less accurate its dating, so that various authorities differ greatly in their estimates. All are agreed, however, on the enormous length of geological time.

It is very difficult to form any real idea of the duration of geological time, particularly if we compare it with the

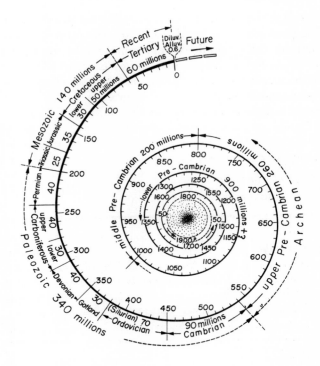

FIG. 1. Time Spiral. (After D. White.)

relatively short span of human history (Fig. 1). Peyer once said that if we compare geological time with one calendar year, the presence of anthropoids (about 600,000 years) would account for the last two and one-half hours of that year, and that of *Homo sapiens* (100,000 years) for the last half hour. Man's recorded history (6,000 years) would correspond to the last one and one-half minutes of our year, and the life of an octogenarian to the last one and one-fifth seconds.

We might add that in Peyer's "geological year"—representing 2,000,000,000 years—the Cambrian period began some time in the middle of September, while bituminous coal was laid down in the middle of November. The first mammal appeared toward the end of November, and the present generation of men made their entry a fraction of a second before the New Year was rung in.

GEOLOGICAL CALENDAR I

Geological Formations and the Development of Vertebrates	*Age in millions of years*

Cenozoic

Quaternary:

Holocene (Recent): Mesolithic and Neolithic (Stone Ages). Discovery of metals opening up modern technology.

Pleistocene (Ice Age): Appearance of man. Paleolithic (Old Stone Age).   2.5

Tertiary:

— Pliocene: Decisive period in formation of man. Fossil finds rare.

~ Miocene: Anthropoid apes have reached Europe and Asia.

~ Oligocene: First anthropoid apes in Africa. Eocene: Numerous lemuroids in Europe and Asia.

Paleocene: Explosive development of mammals.   70

Mesozoic

Cretaceous: Extinction of large reptiles. Jurassic: *Archaeopteryx*. Triassic: First mammals.   200

Paleozoic

> Permian: First theromorphs (mammal-like reptiles).
> Carboniferous: Coal deposits. First reptiles.
> Devonian: First amphibians, descended from *Crossopterygii*.
> Silurian: First fishes.
> Cambrian: Only invertebrates known.   550

Algonkian

> First traces of life.   1,100

Archean

> No life on earth.   2,640

(The Cenozoic has been described in such great detail because of its special bearing on Primate history.)

The Differentiation of Vertebrates

During the early history of the earth, the atmosphere was probably made up mainly of ammonia, methane, carbonic acid, and other gases. Electrical discharges were more frequent and more intensive than they are today, ultraviolet radiation was far more important, and the oceans contained much less salt. Recent work has shown how the action of ultraviolet rays and electric discharges on the original atmosphere and ocean may have produced sugars and even amino acids, the building stones of all living matter. Though scientists are now generally agreed that life can spring from inorganic matter, they still argue whether or not it arose on a single occasion.

Animals are usually divided into two large groups—vertebrates and invertebrates. All invertebrates seem to go back to a common original type. Take the case of the small deep-sea snail *Neopilina galatheae,* which was discovered in 1952 at a depth of over 1,100 feet, by a Danish expedition working off southwestern Costa Rica. Since *Neopilina* belongs to a group of animals which apparently disappeared in the Devonian, scientists were most surprised to find a living representative in the twentieth century. Their surprise became even greater when anatomical studies revealed that its segmented structure made *Neopilina* a relative of the arthropods and annelids. It has since become clear that vertebrates (also called Craniata since each has a cranium), *Amphioxus* (which lacks a skull but has a well-developed dorsal chord corresponding to the spinal column of vertebrates), and some other types may all be lumped together as Chordates.

A rudimentary chord is present in *Balanoglossus,* a worm of most peculiar appearance, and in the tunicates, or sea squirts. In its first larval stage, *Balanoglossus* shows a striking morphological correspondence with the first larval stage of echinoderms (Fig. 2). The correspondence can also be demonstrated by biochemical means. We know that muscle energy depends largely on phosphate exchanges. While chordate muscles contain phosphorus creatine, and most invertebrate muscles contain phosphorus arginine, echinoderm muscles contain both.

Fishes belong to a number of structural types whose increasing specialization becomes clear from the study of

FIG. 2. The first larval stage of *Balanoglossus* (left) and of an echidnoderm (right). An adult *Balanoglossus* is shown on top. (After W. K. Gregory.)

successive geological strata. The oldest fishes lack jaws and have a single aperture on the front edge of their skull. This group includes the extinct Paleozoic Ostracodermi and also the extant Cyclostomes (lampreys), which have gradually developed into parasites. Not much later the first true bony fishes appeared. From them the Crossopterygii (Fig. 3) branched off as early as the Devonian. They are related to the lungfishes (Dipnoi) and, like them, started life as fresh-water fishes. Their fins contain osseous elements corresponding to the bones of quadruped limbs. The Crossopterygii probably used their powerful fins to migrate from pool to pool during droughts, discovering land in their search for water.

One group of Crossopterygii took to life in the sea, and so abandoned the chance of evolving towards life on land. This branch includes the genus *Latimeria,* discovered only a few years ago, first in South Africa and then in Madagascar. It might be called a "living fossil," and as such holds the key to anatomical secrets that true fossils never reveal.

The Upper Devonian of Greenland produced the first quadruped—a primitive amphibian. Its skeleton, and particularly its skull, stamp it unmistakably as a descendent of the Crossopterygii. *Ichthyostega* (Fig. 4) was roughly three feet long and is well known from a number of fossils.

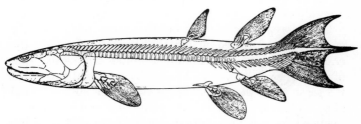

FIG. 3. *Eusthenopteron,* an extinct Crossopterygian from the Devonian of North America. Note the bony elements in the fins. (After W. K. Gregory.)

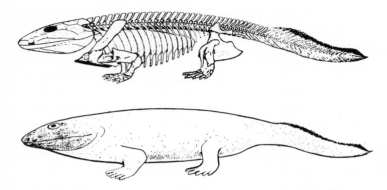

<small>FIG. 4. *Ichthyostega,* from the Devonian of Greenland, the oldest known quadruped. Its cranial and limb structure is reminiscent of that of the Crossopterygii. The animal grew to a length of about 3 feet. (After J. Jarvik.)</small>

Amphibia are rather poorly adapted to life on land. Most need water for propagating their kind. On land they no longer have the support of the surrounding medium, and can only survive by developing stronger limbs and spines. Hence fossil types can be classified by the structure of their vertebrae.

The change from wet-skinned amphibian to dry-skinned and scaly reptile seems to have been very gradual. Opinions still differ whether *Seymouria,* from the Permian of Texas, is a reptile (a cotylosaur) or a somewhat reptilian amphibian.

Of the reptiles we shall only consider the extremely varied Theromorpha ("mammal-like" reptiles). While the cranial roof of the earliest known reptiles was closed, that of some theromorphs was broken by temporal fossae. At the same time, the lower jaw, which originally consisted of many smaller bones, became simplified, and its articular surface began to migrate from the back of the skull to the neighborhood of the ear. Uniform conical teeth made way for a differentiated dentition.

Some Triassic representatives of this group, for example, *Cynognathus* (Fig. 5) must already have shared many mammalian habits. The first true mammal, with a single jaw bone, appeared in the Upper Triassic of Europe.

The paleontologist's demonstration of the close connection between reptiles and mammals came as no surprise to biologists. As early as 1833, Reichert had suggested that the original joint of the reptilian jaw (with articulate and quadrate bones) corresponds to the two mammalian auditory ossicles—the *incus* and *malleus*—and that the single reptilian auditory ossicle—the columella—corresponds to the mammalian *stapes*. (From the early embryonic development of the mammalian skull, we know how the lower jaw in front, and the auditory bones in the back, arise from one and the same element—Meckel's cartilage.)

The "mammal-like" reptiles gave rise to three independent groups of mammals, one of which is extinct. The first living group includes the rare oviparous Monotremata, for example, the Australian platypus and the New Guinea anteater (*Echidna*), whose cloaca has only one posterior aperture. The second group contains all the remaining mammals, namely, all the Marsupialia and the Placentalia or Eutheria—true mammals. The two groups have been distinct since the Jurassic.

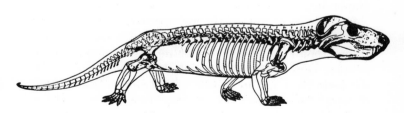

FIG. 5. *Cynognathus,* a mammal-like reptile from the Triassic of South Africa. Bears a strong resemblance to the carnivores. (After C. Camp from W. K. Gregory.)

As we have said, the first mammals appeared in the Upper Triassic. For a long time—the Jurassic and Cretaceous must have lasted for about 100,000,000 years— they remained the size of rats and were overshadowed by the large reptiles. At the end of the Cretaceous, when reptile predominance came to an unexplained end, there was a sudden increase of mammalian forms. The Cenozoic is therefore called the "Age of Mammals." While many strange types still abounded in the Lower Tertiary, the dawn of the Pliocene saw the gradual emergence of the familiar mammalian forms.

Countless fossils help us to reconstruct much of the story of vertebrate evolution. At all times, it was only small groups that managed to achieve a higher degree of organization. The "Age of Fishes" during the Silurian and Devonian was followed by the "Amphibian Age" in the Carboniferous and Permian, by the "Reptilian Age" in the Mesozoic, and by the "Mammalian Age" in the Cenozoic. The total transformation took almost 500,000,000 years. Man appeared at the very end of this period.

Family Trees:
Eohippus into Horse and
Moeritherium into Elephant

Before we examine man's own evolution, we must first look at that of two other mammals. One of them, the horse, may be called the prototype of evolution, since the stages of its development are known in exceptionally great detail.

Modern horses can be divided into three groups: true horses (*Equus*), zebras (*Hippotigris*), and asses (*Asinus*). They are all fairly large animals with one short toe on each foot and with tall columnar teeth. Ancient horses differed radically from the modern species, and it is only from the intermediate stages that we can tell that the two are related at all.

In the Lower Eocene, the primitive hoofed animals of the Lower Tertiary developed into a type with four toes on its front foot and three toes on its hind foot, and with shallow (brachyodont) molars. The original horse, which was probably the size of a fox terrier, appeared simultaneously in Europe (*Hyracotherium*) and in America (*Eohippus*). The European form developed rapidly and split into at least six branches, of which the three-toed *Paleotherium* (European L. Oligocene), resembling the tapir in shape and the rhinoceros in size, is the best known. The original European horse became extinct within a fairly short geological time.

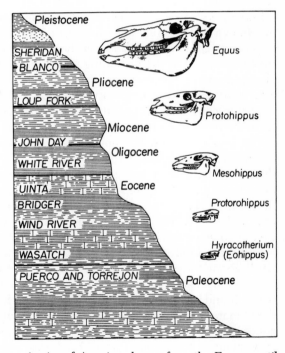

FIG. 6. Increase in size of American horses from the Eocene until modern times. Left: the associated geological formations. (After H. F. Osborn.)

The American *Eohippus* developed into the sheep-sized *Mesohippus* in the Oligocene (Fig. 6). *Mesohippus* had three toes, but only the central toe touched the ground. Its teeth were still brachyodont, but all except the front had assumed the shape of true molars. By the Miocene, American horses had developed into a large number of types with increasingly larger teeth. The pony-sized *Hipparion* reached Europe with a new migrant wave at the beginning of the Pliocene and survived there until the Ice Age. It was still distinctly three-toed, but the lateral toes had become so reduced that they no longer touched the ground. Its teeth were already high-crowned. *Hipparion* so strongly resembled the modern horse that it has been mistaken as its precursor. However, a closer investigation has shown that the real ancestor was *Pliohippus,* another American representative, and that horses migrated to Europe once again at the beginning of the Ice Age. For unknown reasons, horses disappeared from America soon afterward and had to be reimported there by Europeans.

The milestones in the evolution of the horse were, therefore, the marked increase in body size and the reduction of the number of toes. The single toe is so characteristic of the modern horse that it seems farfetched to refer to a three-toed animal by the same name. Anatomists, however, know that the splints of bone present in the foot of the modern horse are vestiges of what were once the second and fourth toes. The change of foot structure was clearly connected with the need for greater speed.

Still more interesting is the specialization of the teeth. Until about the end of the Miocene, the earth was covered mainly with tropical forests, and fodder was therefore soft and juicy. At about the beginning of the Pliocene, the climate became far drier, partly because of the emergence of great mountain ranges. As grassland encroached upon many of the former forests, hard grasses became the staple diet. The teeth were called upon to perform a different function and gradually developed higher crowns.

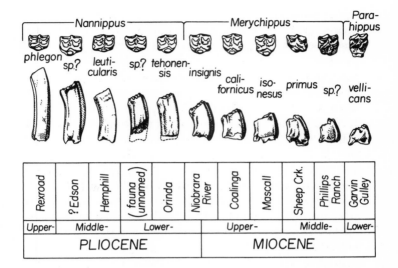

FIG. 7. Absolute increase in height of crowns of a group of North American Mio-Pliocene horses. The degree of specialization increases with time. (After R. A. Stirton.)

From the height of the crown, paleontologists can therefore fix the geological date of fossil horses (Fig. 7) and hence compare and classify fossils from different sites.

The modern horse is separated from the small *Eohippus* by an interval of 50,000,000 years and is by no means a mere copy on a larger scale. The gap between is bridged by intermediate forms. Elephants underwent a similar transformation.

Elephants, whose trunks alone are proof of their high degree of specialization, are the largest living mammals. We distinguish between an Asiatic and an African species, which differ but slightly in structure. Unlike horses, elephants have five-toed feet specially modified to bear their great weight. While we cannot trace the origins of the elephant as far back as those of the horse, we know that its body structure has undergone even more radical modifications in the course of evolution. The oldest known elephants go back to the Middle Eocene of Africa and remained limited to Africa until the Miocene. They were roughly the size of pigs—and were quite different from the modern types. The fossils of the most primitive elephant, *Moeritherium* (so-called after the Egyptian god Moeris), were first discovered in the Fayum basin south of Cairo. Its molars were simple, with two or three ridges, and were clearly distinct from the premolars. The upper jaw still had three incisors on either side and also a small canine. The second incisor was enlarged. The lower jaw had lost one incisor and also the canine. The skull was flattened and laterally elongated and resembled that of primitive sea cows which, despite their greatly reduced limbs (typical of all aquatic mammals), must have shared an ancestor with the elephant. *Moeritherium* was followed by *Phiomia*, also called *Paleomastodon*, which had a much higher skull, one incisor each in the upper and lower jaw, and no canine. Since *Phiomia* was a link between mastodons and true elephants, we know that the tusk of modern elephants is simply an enormously developed second incisor and not an enlarged canine.

At the beginning of the Miocene, the continents were joined by a land bridge, across which mastodons migrated from Africa to Europe, Asia, and America. As a result, the old form split up into a great many new types. Some mastodons grew tusks even in the lower jaw, which became gigantic as a result. Thus a jaw of *Mastodon longirostris* discovered in Rheinhessen was more than six and one-half feet long, and that of *Ambelodon* was longer still. Apparently, the double tusks were so heavy that their owners either became extinct, or else shed their lower ones in time.

The converse happened to *Dinotherium*, an ancient relative of the elephant. Here the lower tusks alone remained, grew larger, and began to turn downward. This branch died out during the Pleistocene.

The teeth of mastodons were well adapted to their functions. While some types had rounded (bunodont) molars for grinding tough food, others had more pointed (tapiroid) teeth, adapted to chewing softer matter. At the same time, the number of transverse molar ridges increased from three to seven or even eight. Mastodons lived on in Europe until the beginning, in Africa until the middle, and in America until the end, of the Ice Age. In South America, the last mastodons were hunted down by the early Peruvians.

In the Lower Pliocene—which also marked a critical point in the history of the horse—the main stage of elephant evolution shifted from Africa to Asia, and a new type of elephant appeared in China. Its molars had up to 14 gable-shaped ridges, and it is therefore called *Stegodon* (*stegos*=roof; *odos*=tooth). In the course of geological time the number of ridges increased even further, while the spaces between them were filled with cement (Fig. 8). The crowns remained low. In India and China, *Stegodon* survived until the middle, and in Java until the end, of the Ice Age. The tusks of some *Stegodon* types reached a length of some 13 feet.

At the end of the Pliocene, this group gave rise to another in which the ridges increased further in number and also in height. The oldest true elephant, the dome-skulled *Elephas planifrons,* was almost indistinguishable from his contemporary, the *Stegodon.* Soon afterward, the elephants developed into two branches. In the Indian branch, which is the more highly specialized, the number of molar ridges reached a maximum of 27. We have seen that the height of horses' teeth can be used for measuring the degree of their evolution. The same is true of elephants' teeth, in which not only the height of the crown but also the number of ridges serve as criteria. While the milk teeth of most mammals are pushed up and out by the premolars beneath them, elephant milk teeth are formed at the back

FIG. 8. Increasing specialization of elephant molars. Top: *Mastodon;* few ridges, little cement. Center: *Stegodon;* more ridges, more cement. Bottom: *Elephas;* still more ridges, clearly separated by cement, and more prominent. All finds from Java.

of the jaw and gradually migrate to the front. During this process, only one or two teeth at a time are functional. The milk teeth persist; all but the oldest elephants lack premolars. The shape of the elephant skull is largely determined by the weight of the heavy tusks which tend to curve it downward.

The large nostrils of elephants are separated by a bridge so fragile that it is often broken off in fossils. Hence an unskilled observer is easily led into mistaking the nasal aperture for the orbit.

All in all, elephants are highly adaptable animals. While they are limited to the tropics today, their woolier Ice Age precursors lived under Arctic conditions. Isolation on islands and inbreeding produced many dwarf types, particularly in Mediterranean regions. A dwarf form was also discovered off the coast of California at Santa Barbara, and a dwarf *Stegodon* in southeastern Asia.

Neither horses nor elephants came into existence before the beginning of the Pleistocene—about 1,000,000 years ago. The modern species are very much more recent—*Equus caballus* appeared in about the middle of the Pleistocene, and the Indian and African elephants cannot be much older than 100,000 years, with a common ancestor in the Lower Pleistocene of Central Africa.

Simpson has shown that horses can be divided into two families with three subfamilies and twenty-six genera, and that their complete evolution from *Eohippus* into *Equus* took place in America.

His classification of elephants into three suborders of five families and twenty-two genera has now replaced Osborn's more complicated system of eight families and twenty-two genera.

The stegodont mastodons of the Lower Pliocene of China were the ancestors of the oldest of all Stegodons, *Stegodon zdanskyi,* which appeared more than 10,000,000 years ago. The change must have taken place in China, although the original center of mastodon development was

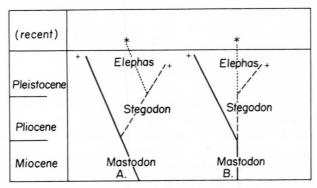

FIG. 9. Two (simplified) methods of illustrating the elephant family tree. A. Each group considered as a separate entity. B. Linear development of the "elephant." Note that the three groups, which developed at different times, occur together in the Pleistocene.

the Lower Tertiary of Africa. The first true elephant— *Elephas planifrons*—appeared in India at the end of the Pliocene, i.e., roughly 1,000,000 years ago.

The relationship between *Stegodon* and *Elephas,* considered as subfamilies, can be illustrated in two ways (Fig. 9):

On the left diagram, every group is represented separately by a straight line. On the right diagram, *Elephas* is considered as a direct descendent of *Mastodon,* with new groups branching off at the end of the Pliocene and of the Miocene respectively. On paper this looks like a sudden break, but in reality the transition was smooth, for each family contained both static and dynamic forms. In other words, all members of a given genus or family are not necessarily on an evolutionary par. It is precisely this difference which explains the wealth of forms in nature. Many adaptations that prove useful in the short run are unable to cope with changes of climate or habitat, and may cause the extinction of a species and sometimes of an entire genus. Moreover, the rate of evolution may vary from group to group, and geographical isolation may easily lead to the survival of lower types. While "high" and "low" are admittedly subjective terms, it cannot be denied that, for instance, a mammal is more highly developed than a fish, even though both are ideally adapted to their respective environments, or that a complex nervous system represents an advance over a simple one.

II. THE PRIMATES

Two hundred years ago, Linnaeus was the first to classify man together with the apes as primates. He has since been proved right by anatomical, physiological, embryological, and serological investigations, even though the term "primates" has been given a different meaning.

Animals are classified according to structure into different categories, of which the smallest is the species. Simpson has distinguished no less than 21 such categories, but the only ones we shall be using here are (in decreasing order):

Superfamily,
　　Family,
　　　　Genus,
　　　　　　Subgenus,
　　　　　　　　Species,
　　　　　　　　　　Subspecies.

Though these terms are used by all zoologists, they do not always refer to the same things.

The primates can be divided into two main groups:
　　the Prosimii (Lemuroids and Tarsioids)
　　and the Anthropoidea (Apes).

Some modern zoologists (Romer, Simpson) have classified the Southeast Asian tree-shrews (Tupaioids) as prosimians, but most others prefer to fit them into the insectivores. All are agreed, however, that the primitive primates were closely related to the insect-eaters.

The largest prosimian group is that of the lemuroids, a few species of which can still be found in Southeastern Asia and in Central and Southern Africa. They are particularly widespread in Madagascar, where one species, the aye-aye, was previously misclassified as a rodent and misnamed *Chiromys* because of its rodent-like teeth. Today the aye-aye is considered to be the last highly specialized representative of a particular lemuroid branch which probably included the extinct European plesiadapids. The Ceylonese loris (Fig. 10) and a number of African species form another special group of lemuroids.

For the problem of human evolution, the most important primates are the tarsioids, the only extant genus of which, *Tarsius* (Fig. 11), lives in Borneo and the Philippines. It is about the size of a small squirrel, has a long tail, a short snout, and, being a nocturnal animal, disproportionately large eyes. Its nails are large and flattened, and it moves about by jumping on its long hindlegs. Its placenta is formed so much like that of the higher apes, that *Tarsius* is considered to be the last descendent of a group of prosimians which share a common precursor with Anthropoidea.

A large number of prosimian fossils (mainly jaws and teeth) have been dug up from the Lower Tertiary of Europe and America. In Europe, prosimians are confined to the Paleocene and Eocene—the European Oligocene is completely devoid of primates, but tarsoids, a group about which little is known but of great phylogenetic interest, are represented by a whole series of genera. They include *Necrolemur,* fairly common in France, and *Microchoerus* of France and England. *Microchoerus* had the

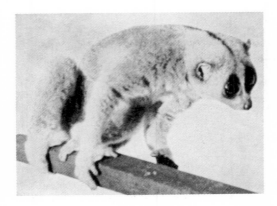

FIG. 10. The slow loris (*Nyctice-bus*), an Indonesian prosimian.

FIG. 11. *Tarsius,* a small Indonesian prosimian, is the last living representative of a group from which the higher primates developed in the Lower Tertiary.

FIG. 12. Old World monkeys have a narrow nose (*Macaca,* left), while New World monkeys have broad nostrils (*Cebus,* right). (After W. Le Gros Clark.)

complicated teeth of European tarsioids. The best-known European fossil lemur is *Adapis;* most museums have at least some parts of its skeleton on permanent display.

Among American lemurs the *Notharctus* group is the most important. Species of this group are known from the Pliocene to the middle Eocene. Gregory has shown that this group probably included the ancestors of the South American monkeys, which therefore form a special group having no more than indirect links with the Old World monkeys.

The Anthropoidea were formerly classified by the shape of their nostrils into Platyrhina (broad nostrils) and Catarrhina (narrow nostrils). The former include the New World monkeys and the latter all the Old World monkeys (Fig. 12). Here we shall distinguish the Anthropoidea into:

> *Ceboidea*
> *Oreopithecoidea*
> *Cercopithecoidea*
> *Hominoidea*

The Ceboidea played no role in the history of man, so we need only say that they had a distinct set of three instead of two premolars. The Oreopithecoidea, which died out in the Lower Pliocene, are considered a special family by Schlosser, but not by others.

The Cercopithecoidea, too, are a highly specialized species, quite distinct from man. They include the macaque, baboon, langur, proboscis monkey, and over 200 other species. With very few exceptions they all have tails. The canine, particularly of the males, is generally large, laterally compressed, and sharp as a knife. Because of this gigantic fang, the South African baboon is more dangerous than any carnivore. The molars of the lower and upper jaws are easily distinguished by the ridges across their cusps. Oddly enough, this relatively primitive group has far more highly specialized teeth than the higher apes. Unfortunately we know very little about its ancestry. When the Cercopithecoids first appeared in Europe and Asia during the Lower Pliocene, they looked much like their modern descendants. Older, somewhat more primitive species are known from the Lower Miocene of East Africa, but have not yet been described in the literature.

The family most directly connected with the history of man is that of the tailless man-apes or anthropomorphs. It includes the tiny Malay gibbon, the orangutan of Borneo and Sumatra, and the African chimpanzee and gorilla. With its height of six and a half feet and its weight of over 750 pounds, the gorilla is taller than most men, and much stronger than any. Oddly enough, the direct precursors of the gorilla and the chimpanzee are unknown. Fossil orangutans have been identified from teeth dug up in China, Indo-China, and Java, regions where the animal has since become extinct. The Chinese variety was as tall as the gorilla, and was presumably the ancestor of the Indonesian orangutan, which grew smaller as a result of its isolation on islands and probably underwent many other modifications.

Fossil anthropoid apes are known from India, East Africa, and Europe (Fig. 13). The first to be described (1856) was *Dryopithecus*. The oldest types include the small *Parapithecus* (Lower Tertiary of Egypt), which is often classified as a special family, and the somewhat larger *Propliopithecus*, which is (wrongly?) identified with the gibbon. In this book, we have used Simpson's system of classification (1945), in which men (Hominidae) and apes (Pongidae, previously called Simiidae) are combined with *Parapithecus* into the family of Hominoidea.

Zoologists differ about the number of families and subfamilies into which the Anthropoidea must be distin-

FIG. 13. Anthropoid Apes. From Asia: (a) Orangutan (left female; right old male with pouched cheeks); (b) Gibbon. From Africa: (c) Chimpanzee; (d) Gorilla. (After Le Gros Clark from E. Kuhn.)

guished. Comparing the writings of, for instance, Abel, Heberer, Gregory, Schlosser, and Simpson, we find that there are just about as many systems of classification. The following classification, though far from final, would seem to reflect our present state of knowledge best:

Superfamily: *Hominoidea*
Family: *Parapithecidae*
Family: *Pongidae*
Subfamilies: *Hylobatinae*
Proconsulinae
Ponginae
Gigantopithecinae
Family: *Hominidae*
Subfamilies: *Australopithecinae*
Homininae

The oldest known hominoid remains come from the Oligocene of Egypt, or more precisely from the Fayum basin south of Cairo, and consist chiefly of lower jaws. One of the best known is *Parapithecus* (Fig. 21) whose small canines have misled various authorities into believing that those of modern man must be of very primitive origin. Recent expeditions from Yale University to the area have brought to light several new species, including a skull of *Aegyptopithecus zeuxis* (illustrated in *Scientific American,* December, 1967), of which a complete scientific account has still to be prepared.

The problem of distinguishing between higher primate subfamilies is best illustrated by the case of the Dryopithecinae and the Ponginae. While Simpson classifies all fossil apes (up to *Gigantopithecus*) with the former, and *Gigantopithecus* and all living species with the latter, we think that *Gigantopithecus* must be considered a representative of a special subfamily. Again, while many zoologists have emphasized that the Dryopithecinae cannot be considered as a distinct group, we feel that our present knowledge does not entitle us to make a further subdivision. Hence the Dryopithecinae have been treated as Pongidae.

The Australopithecinae which Abel and Simpson still classified as pongids are now generally described as hominids; Heberer calls them Prehomininae, but "Australopithecinae" is preferable, if only because it was derived from the first-known species. Finally, man and the fossil types related to him are generally grouped together as Homininae (whom Heberer calls Euhomininae).

Human Evolution

As we saw, the primates evolved during the Cenozoic, comprising the Tertiary and a very much shorter Quaternary. Most of the Tertiary was a warm era even in Europe, except toward the end when it made way for the Ice Ages. These are divided into four long glacial periods, with three warmer interglacials between them. The glacials are known by special names based on the Alpine valleys in which their moraines were found. The Würm glacial is further subdivided into three, and the other glacials into at least two, interstadials. Since the glacials correspond to certain radiation minima, resulting from periodic change of distance between the earth and the sun, and also from shifts in inclination between the terrestrial axis and the ecliptic, Milankovitch was able to compute a radiation curve that serves as a kind of geological calendar. The "classical" Ice Age was preceded by a long period of climatic disturbance, the so-called Villafranchian. Fortunately for us, it went hand in hand with marked faunal changes. The true horse, the true elephant, and cattle emerged at the beginning of the Pleistocene and the fauna even of areas not directly affected by the Ice Age can therefore be distinguished from Tertiary fauna. However, since local factors also played an important role, it is not always easy to fit fossil finds into a definite period of the (geologically) short Pleistocene.

Relatively recent geological periods can be dated by two other, quite modern, geological procedures. The foremost of these is the C^{14} method. In building up their carbon compounds by photosynthesis, plants and animals absorb radioactive carbon dioxide, which has a lifetime of 60,000 years. From the radioactive residue, we can therefore calculate the age of relatively recent fossils.

The second method is the analysis of pollen. Pollen, being exceptionally stable, is an excellent guide to the flora to which it once belonged. The pollen method is particularly well suited to the dating of the Pleistocene because large scale changes of vegetation occurred during that period. Due allowance must, of course, be made for differences in latitude and for purely local influences.

No true human fossils are known from before the Pleistocene, and few fossils of any kind from the Upper and

GEOLOGICAL CALENDAR II

The Cenzoic		*Age in Years*
Quaternary:	Holocene (Alluvium)	20,000
	Pleistocene (Diluvium)	
	Würm glaciation	115,000
	last interglacial	
	Riss glaciation	230,000
	"great" interglacial	
	Mindel glaciation	475,000
	first interglacial	
	Günz glaciation	600,000
	"Villafranchian"	2,500,000
Tertiary:	Pliocene	12,000,000
	Miocene	
	Oligocene	
	Eocene	
	Paleocene	70,000,000

Middle Pliocene when erosions were frequent in the Old World. The Lower Pliocene, however, has yielded a rich harvest of nonhuman fossils (see opposite page).

The history of the pongids, like that of the elephants, began in the Oligocene of Africa; only during the Miocene did both reach Europe and Asia. The Old World Pliocene opened with the appearance of the American three-toed horse (*Hipparion*), which initiated a marked change in the fauna of the Old World.

When it comes to man and his relatives, comparative zoologists and anthropologists are able to base much of their work on the study of extant species. They are therefore much better off than paleontologists and paleoanthropologists who have to rely exclusively on skeletons and fragments of skeletons, or even a single tooth. Probability counts and experience have, however, shown that such isolated finds very often represent a "mean value" and may be considered as such, marked differences between them notwithstanding. Man is classified as belonging to the

Order: *Primates*
Suborder: *Anthropoidea*
Tribe: *Catarrhina*
Superfamily: *Hominoidea*
Family: *Hominidae*
Genus: *Homo*
Species: *sapiens*

Quite naturally, there have been many attempts to place man, with his high and very special intelligence, into a category apart. Thus Blumenbach (1737) introduced the term *Bimana,* and Illiger (1811) the term *Erecta.* However, neither man's ambidextrousness nor his erect posture are enough to secure him a special position. More recently, Kählin has suggested that the Hominidae, the Pongidae, and the Parapithecidae be considered as superfamilies, but his system runs counter to all established criteria of classification.

Keith has shown that, of his many anatomical character-istics, man shares

369 with the chimpanzee
385 with the gorilla
354 with the orangutan
117 with the gibbon

and only 113 with the common monkeys. A mere 312 are exclusively man's own.

As we have said, man belongs to the species *Homo sapiens*. Unlike all other species, man has no characteris-tic geographical distribution and no fixed habitat. Again, while weak, sick, and deviating animals have few chances of survival or of propagating their kind, and hence disap-pear to leave a balanced type, and while geographical iso-lation usually produces subspecies which eventually turn into new species, no such thing occurs in man.

Modern man inhabits almost the entire earth. Different races can mix and produce fertile offspring. Weak, sick and even deviating individuals are cared for by the com-munity, while the fittest are the most likely to be killed off in wars. Large groups that would die if left to nature, for instance diabetics, are kept alive by drugs, and may pro-duce large families. Hence human variability is very much greater than that of any other species. In fact, ours is not so much a real species as a conglomeration of individuals.

Zoologists use the binary nomenclature of Linnaeus. The first name (always with an initial capital) designates the genus, the second (with no initial capital) the species. By international agreement, the names of species may not be changed, though a species may be fitted into a different or—if need be—even into a new genus. Anthropologists who are far less strict about nomenclature than zoologists have introduced a great deal of additional confusion. Though there is no doubt that a number of fossil genera and probably also of fossil species had best be omitted altogether, it is still too early to say which are the redundant ones. In general, the names of apes end in *-pithecus* and those of men in *-anthropus*. These endings usually express no more than the opinion of the original discoverer, but are best left unchanged for the time being.

We must guard carefully against projecting the present into the past. There may be only one particular species today, but we cannot conclude that more never existed. Thus one and the same layer from the Lower Miocene of East Africa contained three species of *Proconsul* together with (at least) one species of *Sivapithecus* and two species of *Limnopithecus*. From the older Chinyi layers of the Indian Siwaliks we know seven, from the more recent Nagri layers eleven, and from the Dhok Pathan layers three different species of pongid. Most species are restricted to a single layer; no more than two species seem to share the Chinyi and Nagri layers. Though some of these species may have been "synonymous," they nevertheless had marked differences. Experience has taught us, and not only in the case of the pongids, that different strata often reflect a change of fauna from which, indeed, we distinguish the strata in the first place. As a result, animals of different geological age are legitimately classified as different species. Thus *Pithecanthropus erectus* and *Pithecanthropus modjokertensis* of Java were rightly distinguished from each other long before more recent finds enabled students to determine the real differences between them. To have ignored the geological interval between these two species, and to have considered their differences negligible when compared with the variability of modern man, would have been a clear mistake. Fossils also suggest that a number of human species—much more clearly distinct from one another than modern races—must have lived side by side in the Pleistocene. The older a species, the smaller its variability and geographical distribution.

Paleontologists may be accused of having erected their edifice on very flimsy foundations. However, minor gaps

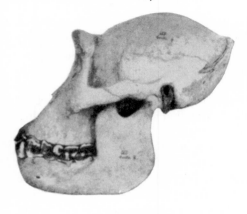

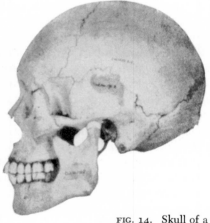

FIG. 14. Skull of a female gorilla (upper) and of modern man (lower), seen from the side. (F. Weidenreich.)

and errors apart, they can rightly claim that the building itself is quite firm, though the rooms themselves are unfinished.

Before we go any further, we must first explain by what characteristics or group of characteristics man's evolution can be compared with that of the higher apes. We need not dwell on the gibbons, for they are adapted to a special life in tropical treetops, and further, do not differ enough from the other apes to warrant a special discussion.

Let us begin with the skull. Figure 14 shows that, whereas the gorilla has a small cranium and a large face, and whereas it is prognathous (having projecting jaws), man's cranium is larger than his face, and he is orthognathous (straight-jawed). Again, modern man lacks the continuous brow ridge (*torus supraorbitalis*) of the apes, and even primitive man had his ridge interrupted over the base of the nose. Behind their eyes, anthropoid apes have a characteristic postorbital constriction. Again, the condyle of their lower jaw fits into a shallow groove, which is separated from the ear by the process postglenoidalis. Man lacks this process, but has a deeper groove and a mastoid process behind the ear. This process is either absent or very small in all apes. Unlike man, the back of whose skull is rounded, apes have an occipital crest. Their foramen magnum (through which the spinal cord passes to be continuous with the brain) emerges at an angle from the back of the skull, whereas in man it runs straight down from the center. Man's skull is more evenly balanced on the vertebral column.

On top of the skull lie the temporal grooves to which the muscles moving the lower jaw were once attached. These grooves meet in the males of all three anthropoid apes and exceptionally in the female gorilla, but never in man. Again, the skull of anthropoid apes is strengthened with a bony crest to support the heavy jaw muscles. In the gorilla the crest may protrude a few centimeters. The size of the brain case depends on the cranial capacity, which is smaller in apes than in man both absolutely and also relatively. Female apes generally have a somewhat smaller cranial capacity than the males. The largest cranial capacity measured in an anthropoid ape was 685 cc. (in a male gorilla). Besides being much larger, the human brain also has many more convolutions. The

brain to body weight ratios of man and anthropoid apes to
each other are roughly as 4:1.

BRAIN CAPACITY OF MAN AND ANTHROPOID APES

(mean values)

Man	1,350–1,500 cc.
Gorilla	350– 685 cc.
Orangutan	295– 575 cc.
Chimpanzee	320– 480 cc.

(After Hagedorn quoting Gieseler)

The smaller brain capacity in apes is reflected in their
low and receding foreheads. As we shall see, the high brow
of man is a recent development, absent in even his direct
ancestors, and varying from race to race.

The most common fossils are the teeth, which keep better than any other part of the skeleton. They are also far
less variable than other parts, and paleontologists have
therefore reconstructed many types of animals from their
teeth alone. The most important work in this field was
done by W. K. Gregory.

The normal permanent teeth of placental mammals consist of three incisors (I), one canine (C), four premolars
(P), and three molars (M) in each half of the jaw. In the
higher primates, the milk canines and milk incisors are
generally smaller, and the milk molars (d) generally larger
than the permanent teeth which they precede. In all
hominoidea, the premolars and molars are morphologically
distinct, and the last milk molar generally bears a striking
resemblance to the first permanent molar.

In all higher apes, reduction of the number of teeth has
led to the loss of the lateral incisor and of the two front
premolars. Hence every half of each jaw contains eight
teeth. Molars are usually numbered from the front to the
back; hence M_3 is the most posterior. A fourth or super-
numerary molar is found fairly frequently in the orang-

utan, and very exceptionally in man. It results from a division of the tooth germ. Premolars, too, are numbered from the front to the back; P_4 is therefore the most posterior and P_3 the most anterior—P_2 and P_1 have been lost. Unfortunately, this method of numbering teeth, introduced by paleontologists, is not always used by other scholars, and a great deal of confusion results. Thus many anatomists (for instance Weidenreich) count the teeth from the front (P_1) to the back (P_2) and make no allowance for those that have been lost in the course of evolution. Others again (e.g., Hürzeler), while also making no allowance for lost teeth, count them from the back to the front, calling the back premolar P_1 and the front premolar P_2.

The molars of mammals can be traced back to a basic tritubercular (three-cusped) type. Though vastly changed over the ages, they can still be recognized in the upper molars of the modern hominoidea (Fig. 15). The forces

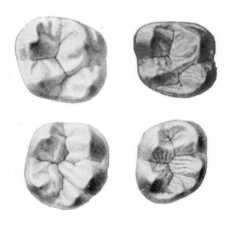

FIG. 15. The basic similarity between the dental pattern of man (left) and of the chimpanzee (right). First right upper molar (top) and first right lower molar (bottom). Twice natural size. (After E. Selenka.)

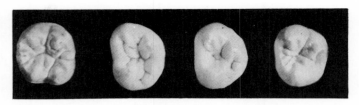

FIG. 16. Change of dental pattern of human upper molars from four to three cusps. 1½ times natural size.

which influence the teeth act from the front to the back; the original pattern is therefore best preserved in the first molar. In apes, the largest molar is usually the second in the upper and the third in the lower jaw; in modern man the largest molar in either jaw is the first.

Upper molars have four main cusps, of which the two outer and the front inner correspond to the original three of the basic type, the so-called trigon. The inner and back outer cusps often remain joined by the original transverse ridge (*crista transversa*) which, in hominoidea, invariably ends on the tip, and in *Oreopithecus* on the anterior edge, of the back cusp. The back inner cusp (hypocone) arose from the basal cingulum, surrounding the original trigon; it is usually the least prominent of the four (see Fig. 16). Lower molars have five undulating cusps—two inner and three outer. These cusps are distinguished from their counterparts in the upper molars by the suffix -*id*. Only the two front cusps stem from the original trigonid. They are frequently joined by a ridge. The third cusp of the trigonid may occur very exceptionally in the lower milk teeth, but has generally disappeared. On the extreme back edge of the lower molar lies the hypoconulid, which is strongly developed in hominoidea.

Men and anthropoid apes share the main cusp pattern of their upper and lower molars, but differ slightly in the formation of the cusps, and in the ridges between them. These ridges are most prominent in the gorilla. The orang-

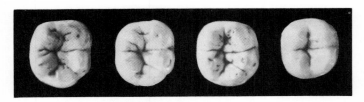

FIG. 17. Change of dental pattern of human lower molars from five to four cusps. Left: typical "Dryopithecus pattern." 1½ times natural size.

utan has a typically low and flat crown covered with very many fine enamel wrinklings.

In man, the four cusps of particularly the second and third upper molars are often reduced to three, and the five cusps of the lower molars to four. Australian aborigines generally retain five cusps on all three molars of the lower jaw. Between the two back cusps there often appears a very small sixth cusp, the *tuberculum sextum.*

In the original lower molar, the front inner cusp (the so-called metaconid) made broad contact with the central outer cusp (the hypoconid). This pattern is highly characteristic of all hominoidea. It was first found in a Miocene group and was called the "Dryopithecus pattern" by Gregory and Hellman. It is expressed by the formula 5Y, indicating that it has five cusps, between which a system of oblique and transverse grooves range round a central Y. 5Y gradually developed into 4+, i.e., a system of four cusps with + shaped grooves (see Fig. 17). The first molar of most modern men still shows traces of the Dryopithecus pattern; the second is quadritubercular. In monkeys, all the molars are almost invariably quadritubercular, and the summits of the opposite cusps are linked by prominent transverse crests. This type of molar, which is more highly specialized than the one we have been describing, is called bilophodont (double-crested). In many species, the last molar of the lower jaw still has a very large fifth cusp.

With *Oreopithecus* we meet yet another type of dentition. Here the back inner cusp of the upper molar is joined by a ridge to another, oblique, ridge (the *crista obliqua*). The lower first and second molars have four main cusps and a rudimentary hypoconulid. In many monkeys the back molars are greatly elongated.

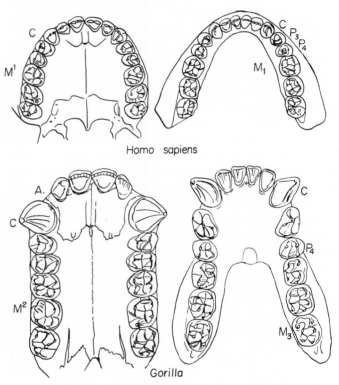

FIG. 18. Characteristic differences between dental arch and proportions of teeth in man and anthropoid apes. Man has a rounded and closed dental arch, small canines (C) and premolars (P), and prominent first molars (M_1). Anthropoid apes (often) have parallel rows of teeth, typical "monkey gaps" (diastemata), and large canines and premolars. The largest molar of monkeys is the last (M_3) in the lower jaw and the one but last (M_2) in the upper jaw. (Partly after W. K. Gregory.)

FIG. 19. Correspondence in the structure of the first lower premolar (P₃) of a primitive hominid (*Sinanthropus*, top), and of a chimpanzee (below). Outer, inner, and front views. 1½ times natural size. (After F. Weidenreich.)

The hominoidea can be distinguished not only by their basically identical molar patterns, but also by the shape of their canines, which affects the shape of the lower front premolars and hence the entire shape of the dental arch. All types with large canines have two gaps (*diastemata*) between their upper teeth, into which the lower canines fit when the jaw is closed. These "monkey-gaps" are present in all pongids but are absent in man, who has very small canines and a continuous dental arch (Fig. 18).

Discussions of the origins of man invariably introduce the canine problem. It appears that the oldest pongids from the Oligocene of Africa still had small or fairly small canines. Hence a great many students have concluded that man's small canine is a primitive characteristic. On the other hand, Remane has shown that the special characteristics of man's lower milk tooth can only be explained if one assumes the existence of a large original canine. We shall see later what light fossil discoveries have thrown on this discussion.

As a result of canine specialization, the first lower premolar of pongids frequently assumes a monocuspid form, unlike man's, which is bicuspid. However, since a second cusp is found in such pongids as the chimpanzee (Fig. 19), particularly in the milk teeth, this distinction cannot be a fundamental one.

Man's lower jaw comes to a point (the chin) bearing a small bone process, the *spina mentalis,* to which the muscles of the tongue are attached. This process is missing in

apes. The three existing anthropoid apes (but not the gibbon) still have a bony shelf (the "simian shelf") which
stretches across from one side of the lower jaw to the
other below the chin. The two lower halves of the jaw
meet in a symphysis, by whose cross section different
species can be identified.

Differences in the rest of the skeleton can be treated
briefly because of the great scarcity of fossil material. We
know that the humerus and femur of pongids are of equal
length, whereas modern man has a longer femur. Man's
erect posture has led to a shortening of his pelvis and to a
broadening of his ossa ilii to take the greater weight of his
upright body. Hands and feet of man and apes differ in
degree of development rather than in basic form—the foot
of the mountain gorilla is fairly similar to that of man.

Though modern primates have similar body structures,
their physical proportions vary a great deal (Fig. 20). Unfortunately, we know little about these proportions in fossil
men and apes.

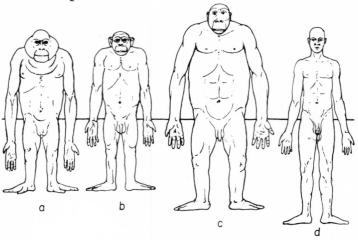

FIG. 20. Proportions of anthropoid apes and of man (d). (a) Orangutan; (b) Chimpanzee; (c) Gorilla. (After A. Schultz from H.
Kuhn.)

III.   FOSSIL ANTHROPOID APES

The first hominoid family—the Parapithecidae—contains only one species.

> *Parapithecus* Schlosser, 1911. Lower jaw only. Very small type (length of three lower molars: 12.5 mm.). Canines and incisors small, hence marked convergence of teeth towards the front. Both premolars monocuspid. Rami of lower jaw slope backwards. Lower Oligocene of Egypt.

Schlosser correctly described *Parapithecus fraasi* (Fig. 21) as a representative of a distinct family, but on the false assumption that it still had three premolars and only one incisor. Nowadays, *Parapithecus* is placed in a distinct category because of extremely primitive characteristics which make it a probable link between the higher apes and the Cercopithecinal monkeys. Because of the marked convergence of its teeth, the incomplete ossification of its symphysis, and the slope of the rami of its jaw, *Parapithecus* has a striking resemblance to the lemurs.

The family of the Pongidae (previously known as the Simiidae) cannot be easily classified. Of the existing types, the gibbons (Hylobatidae) are often treated as a special family. They must be considered an overspecialized group, not only because of their exceptionally long limbs, but also because of their exceptionally large canines (present in both sexes). Their fossil history is not well known. The first definite gibbons of the modern type were discovered in the Pleistocene of Southern China and Java.

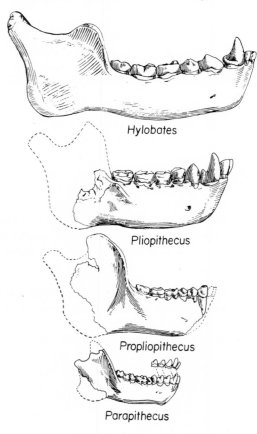

FIG. 21. Lower jaws of *Parapithecus* and *Propliopithecus* from the lower Pliocene of Egypt compared with lower jaws of *Pliopithecus* from the Miocene of France and of a modern gibbon (*Hylobates*). ¾ natural size. (After W. K. Gregory.)

The Hylobatidae, and probably all anthropoid apes in general, must have descended from *Propliopithecus* (Fig. 21), discovered in the same layers as *Parapithecus*.

> *Propliopithecus* Schlosser, 1911. Only lower jaw known. Small shape (length of row of molars 15.0 mm.). Front premolars monocuspid, back premolars bicuspid. Distinct canine. Tooth pattern simple, hypoconulid still central. Lower Oligocene of Egypt.
>
> *Oligopithecus savagei* Simons, 1962.
>
> *Aegyptopithecus zeuxis* Simons, 1963.
>
> *Aelopithecus chirobates* Simons, 1963, discovered by Professor Simons of Yale in the Oligocene of Fayum. Lower jaw only, rather small; relationship to other primates uncertain.

Propliopithecus haeckeli clearly represents an advance over *Parapithecus*, since its back premolar is bicuspid like that of all higher apes. Its front (permanent and milk) molar is monocuspid like that of the gibbon. We cannot tell whether this is a primary or secondary characteristic (resulting from enlarged canines).

The following may be considered as fossil Hylobatidae:

> *Limnopithecus* Hopwood, 1933. Gibbon-sized; slender lower jaws; front premolar monocuspid; very long limb bones. Lower Miocene of East Africa.
>
> *Prohylobates* Fourteau, 1920. Only lower jaw known. Classification doubtful. Lower Miocene of Egypt.
>
> *Hispanopithecus* Villalta and Crusafont, 1944. Teeth without wrinkles; front premolar monocuspid. Lower Pliocene of Spain.
>
> *Bunopithecus* Matthew and Granger, 1923. Probably related to, or identical with, the large gibbon (*Symphalangus*) of Sumatra. Pleistocene of Southern China.
>
> *Hylobates* (and *Symphalangus*). Pliocene of Mongolia; "*Pliopithecus*"—Pleistocene of Southern China and Java.

Next we shall consider the pongids and first of all the existing large anthropoid apes. Unfortunately, we know nothing about the Pleistocene ancestry of either the gorilla or the chimpanzee (*Anthropopithecus*), and little about their possible relationship with Tertiary European types. The only species whose prehistory is known to any extent is the orangutan (*Pongo*).

> *Palaeosimia* Pilgrim, 1915. Known only from an upper molar (Fig. 22), whose enamel folds and wrinkles foreshadow that of the orangutan. Lower Pliocene of Pakistan.

> *Pongo* (*Simia*). Only isolated fossilized teeth. The Southern China Pleistocene type resembled the gorilla in size. Hence the extant species in Borneo and Sumatra must have grown smaller as a result of isolation. Other modifications include a shortened skull and small brow ridges. Also found in the Pleistocene of Indo-China. The teeth of recent types are indistinguishable from those discovered in the Pleistocene of Java. Subrecent in Middle Sumatra.

Another, heterogeneous, group contains the fossil *Dryopithecus* (the first-known type) and other fossil types that are sometimes considered as a special subfamily. This distinction strikes us as pointless.

> *Dryopithecus* Lartet, 1856. Large to very large canines; dental pattern relatively simple; lower molars have typical *Dryopithecus* pattern. Possibly in Lower Miocene of East Africa; Lower Miocene of Egypt; Middle and Upper Miocene of Europe; Lower Pliocene of the Siwaliks (Fig. 23) and of China. The European *Dryopithecus fontani* (Austria, France) is possibly related to the gorilla.

> *Sivapithecus* Pilgrim, 1910. According to Pilgrim, the lower molars (Fig. 24) resemble those of man; large canines. Lower and Middle Pliocene of the Siwaliks.

FIG. 22. Tooth germ of a first upper molar, described as *Dryopithecus germanicus*. Possibly of *Paidopithex*. From the Lower Pliocene of Salmendingen, Swabia. Original in Tübingen Museum. Three times natural size. (W. Molison.)

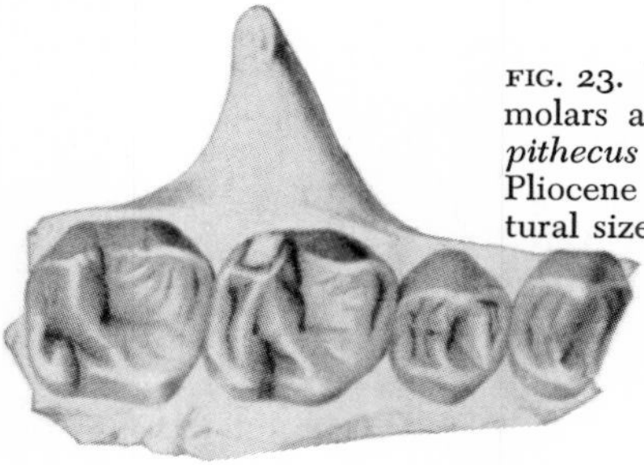

FIG. 23. Upper jaw fragment with two molars and three premolars of *Dryopithecus punjabicus* from the Lower Pliocene of the Siwaliks. 1½ times nattural size. (After G. Pilgrim.)

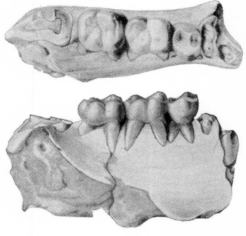

FIG. 24. Lower jaw fragment with two molars and one premolar of *Sivapithecus indicus* from the Lower Pliocene of the Siwaliks. Natural size. (After G. Pilgrim.)

The last two species are the only ones with a wide geo-graphical distribution. (The Siwalik Hills are famous mammalian deposits in the Himalayan foothills, now shared between India and Pakistan.) Purely European genera are:

Pliopithecus Gervais, 1849. Small type. Classi-fied as a hylobatid, until Zapfe's discovery of nu-merous skeleton bones showed to be a pongid of a special type. Widely distributed in the Miocene of Europe (Czechoslovakia, Austria, Germany, France, Switzerland).

Paidopithex Pohlig, 1895. Originally recon-structed from a slender but enlarged gibbon-like femur, first discovered in 1820 (Eppelsheim). Teeth also known from the Swabian bean-ore; a lower jaw from Lerida is more arched than that of *Dryopithecus fontani*. Teeth partly resemble the chimpanzees'. Lower Pliocene of Germany and Spain.

Rhenopithecus von Koenigswald, 1956. Smaller than *Paidopithex* from the same strata. Only one molar. Lower Pliocene of Germany (Rheinhessen).

Austriacopithecus Ehrenberg, 1938. Known only from a few skeleton bones which are reminiscent of lower apes. Probably identical with Dryopithe-cus. Miocene of Austria.

In addition, there are the following Asiatic types:

Ankarapithecus Ozansoy, 1957. Known only from one worn-down lower jaw. Large type. Lower Pliocene of Turkey.

Palaeopithecus Lydekker, 1879. Reconstructed from a well-preserved upper jaw. Large canines. Probably related to the gorilla. Middle Pliocene of Siwalik.

Indopithecus von Koenigswald, 1951. Very large type. Lower molars strongly wrinkled. Lower Pliocene of Siwalik.

Bramapithecus Lewis, 1934. Small type. Lower teeth partly shortened. Lower Pliocene of Siwalik.

Sugrivapithecus Lewis, 1934. Small type. Teeth fairly unwrinkled. First premolar enlarged. Lower Pliocene of Siwalik.

Ramapithecus Lewis, 1934. Small type. Small gap in upper jaw. Small canines. Lower front premolar bicuspid. Upper Pliocene of Siwalik, possible precursor of hominoids.

The remaining fossil forms can be fitted into two further subfamilies:

Proconsul Hopwood, 1933. Size halfway between small chimpanzee and gorilla. Skull of *Proconsul africanus* without brow ridges and with brain convolutions reminiscent of lower apes. Dental pattern very complicated. Upper molars almost completely enclosed in basal cingulum. Lower Miocene of East Africa (Figs. 25–27).

Proconsul has so distinct a set of upper molars that it is apparently unconnected with the history of man.

FIG. 25. *Proconsul*—site on the island of Rusinga in Lake Victoria, Kenya.

We have classified *Gigantopithecus blacki* as belonging to a special subfamily. It is a gigantic hominoid which, despite its size, generally lacks canines and has bicuspid first premolars. This is particularly true of the females. Because of the presence of central hypoconulids, the molars were probably more primitive than those of *Dryopithecus*.

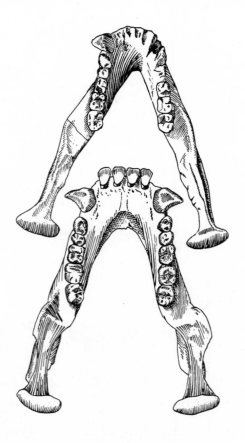

FIG. 26. Lower jaw of *Proconsul nyanzae* (top) from the lower Miocene of Rusinga and of chimpanzee (below). The second jaw, unlike the first, has a simian shelf. (After W. Le Gros Clark.)

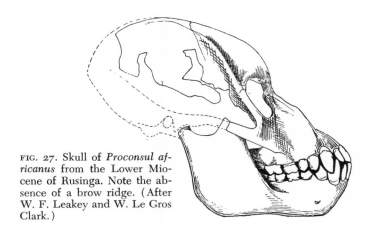

FIG. 27. Skull of *Proconsul africanus* from the Lower Miocene of Rusinga. Note the absence of a brow ridge. (After W. F. Leakey and W. Le Gros Clark.)

Gigantopithecus von Koenigswald, 1935. Largest of the higher primates. Originally known from a few teeth discovered in Chinese pharmacies. From 1956, lower jaws have been dug up in Southern China. Canines smaller than those of existing anthropoid apes. Despite its large size, *Gigantopithecus* had more "manlike" teeth than any living anthropoid ape (Fig. 28). Ancient and Middle Pleistocene of Southern China.

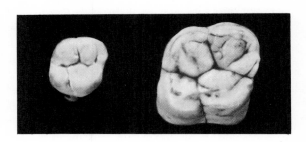

FIG. 28. Upper molar of *Gigantopithecus* compared with that of man. About 1½ times natural size.

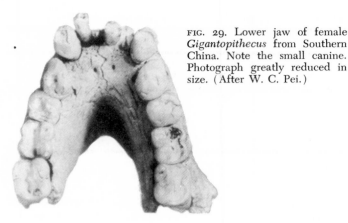

FIG. 29. Lower jaw of female *Gigantopithecus* from Southern China. Note the small canine. Photograph greatly reduced in size. (After W. C. Pei.)

A lower jaw recently dug up by Pei in a cave near Liu-Cheng, Kwangsi, South China (Jaw III) is by far the largest jaw of any higher fossil primate (Fig. 29). According to Pei, the height of the tip of the jaw is 101.5 mm. (Gorilla: 60.7 mm.), its thickness is 47.0 mm. (Gorilla: 18 mm.), and the length of the three molars is 59.2 mm. (Gorilla: 50.2 mm.). From these figures, we may take it that *Gigantopithecus* was larger than the gorilla.

Because of its dental pattern, *Gigantopithecus* was described as a gigantic hominid by Weidenreich, and Weinert not only changed its name to *Giganthropus*, but has also reconstructed its lower jaw according to that of Heidelberg man. Neither view is acceptable.

Paleontological distinctions between genera of fossil anthropoid apes are based on extremely limited material. As a result, the definitions of different species, let alone of different genera, are rather vague. Though the close to ten distinct species of *Dryopithecus* cannot really all belong to the same genus, no better classification has yet been suggested. What large gaps there are in our picture emerges clearly from the following table:

Distribution of fossil and recent pongids

	Africa	Asia	Europe
Recent	*Gorilla* *Anthropopithecus*	*Pongo* (*Hylobates*)	
Pleistocene		*Pongo* *Gigantopithecus* (*Bunopithecus*) (*Hylobates*)	
Upper Pliocene		*Sugrivapithecus* *Bramapithecus* *Palaeopithecus* *Ankarapithecus*	(*Hispanopithecus*)
Lower Pliocene		*Indopithecus* *Sivapithecus* *Dryopithecus*	*Rhenopithecus* *Paidopithex*
Upper Miocene	*Kenyapithecus* (*Prohylobates*)	*Kansupithecus*	*Dryopithecus* *Austriacopithecus*
Lower Miocene	*Dryopithecus* "*Sivapithecus*" *Proconsul* (*Limnopithecus*)		*Pliopithecus*
Upper Oligocene	*Aegyptopithecus* *Aelopithecus* *Oligopithecus*		
Lower Oligocene	*Propliopithecus* *Parapithecus*		

(*In parenthesis: probable hylobatids.*)

During the past few years there have been several attempts to classify fossil pongids based on population studies of entire taxa, which naturally have a greater variability than clearly defined species. Our reservations about the new approach are due to the fact that the material is too sparse and that primate jaws alone do not provide an adequate basis for firm conclusions. Thus, when Simons and Pilbeam (1962) use an upper molar from the Lower Miocene of Kenya, two from the Middle

Miocene, and one from the Lower Pliocene of Europe
to conclude that they have discovered the same variability
as obtains in the modern chimpanzee, they go much too
far—all they have really proved is that the dentition has
remained remarkably constant, not the animal as a whole.
Had they used the same approach in studying the evolution of the horse, the elephant, the dog, the bear, or the
hyena (the latter was not yet present in the Miocene) the
results would have been quite different. And why should
the higher primates have been less dynamic and adaptable than their contemporaries? On that assumption, man
would never have seen the light of day. How, in fact, is it
possible that a species (or taxon) ranging from Africa
south of the Sahara through Europe to Central China
should have remained static from the Lower Miocene to
the Middle Pliocene for more than 10 million years? If,
when dealing with a group as responsive to its environment as the higher primates certainly are—a group which,
as the wide variey of Africa and Asia and the many
species and races of gibbons in Southeast Asia prove, has
a marked tendency to produce new species—we do not
make a sharp distinction between forms from different
environments and strata, then we shall never be able to
reconstruct the natural groups (the great variability of
modern forms does not affect the issue in the least).
Thus whenever we discover the remains of two primates
in two successive strata, each with its own fauna, it is
far more likely that we have dug up two species rather
than one. That is precisely why we cannot agree to the
classification of Lewis and Pilbeam, which, incidentally,
they themselves have described as "provisional." Simons
and Pilbeam admit the existence of only four species in
Asia and Europe, namely *Dryopithecus fontani, Dryopithecus laitanus, Dryopithecus indicus,* and *Dryopithecus
sivalensis.* They completely ignore the distinction between Miocene (Sarmatic) and Pliocene (Pontic) forms,
between forest and steppe inhabiting, and Indian and

European types. This, we believe, is not an acceptable procedure, though we readily grant that some kind of revision of the existing classification is overdue.

All the authors we have cited are in agreement on the precise status of only one family, namely the extinct Parapithecidae, recently the subject of new discoveries by Simons. The gibbons present further difficulties—they used to be treated as a special family, particularly by Abel and Heberer. More recently, Chiarelli (1966) has shown that *Hylobates,* like certain Cercopithecines, has 44 chromosomes, while anthropoid apes have 48 and man has 46. From a detailed study by Ankel (1964) of the sacrum of *Pliopithecus,* which has always been treated as a fossil gibbon, it appears that this animal must have had a long tail, something no hominoid is supposed to have. *Pliopithecus* must therefore be fitted into a separate family closer to the Cercopithecoidea than to the Hominoidea, more so since the molars of the former are bilophodont (double-crested), a form of specialization that can be traced back to Hylobates. As early as 1892, Kohlbrügge stressed that anthropoids and hylobatids were not "successive stages but parallel forms."

The Proconsulinae, an ancient African group, have a primitive build and such unusual (probably overspecialized) teeth, that they must be treated as a separate subfamily (Heberer's view), and perhaps even as a distinct family.

In short, the higher primates must have emerged in Africa during the Lower Oligocene; there are no fossils from the Upper Oligocene, the Upper Miocene, the entire Pliocene, or even the Pleistocene of that continent.

In Asia, the Miocene is poorly represented, but the Lower and Middle Pliocene have yielded rich harvests from the Chinji and Nagri zones of the Siwaliks.

As we have said, the oldest pongids were discovered in Africa. In Europe, they first occur, together with mastodons, in the Upper Miocene. Since they must have reached Asia at about the same time, no earlier pongids are likely to be discovered there. For this reason we doubt whether some inconclusive fossils from the Eocene of Burma, classified respectively as *Pondaungia* and *Amphipithecus* (the latter with three premolars), are correctly described as Pongidae.

The connection between the pongids and man can be inferred, first of all, from molar resemblances. The molars of *Paidopithex* were originally classified as *Dryopithecus* sp. by Branco in 1898. Branco mentioned that the two molars were first described in 1850 by Jäger who, apparently, took them, not for fossil, but for recent alluvial human teeth. One of them, a lower molar, "was sent to R. Owen in London, who agreed that it was undoubtedly a human tooth. . . ." Professor Arnold of Tübingen, the anatomist, made a similar pronouncement on teeth of the same kind, which had meanwhile been acquired by Quenstedt. It appeared that they resembled the third molar of Mongols, Finns, and Moors.

As we can see, paleontologists base their classifications chiefly on the canine-premolar section of the jaw, which is far too frequently missing. Added to this is the difficulty that no one is quite certain of the form of the original human canine. Hence types with large canines are far too readily classified as pongids, on the unwarranted assumption that the teeth of modern apes can be used as a general criterion.

Sivapithecus was said by Pilgrim to be related to man, but its large canines make this classification doubtful. In 1938, Freudenberg had this to say of *Giganthropus weinheimensis* from the Lower Pliocene of Rheinhessen: "The much-sought-for Tertiary man has at last been found, far from the limits of the Diluvium." From his sketchy diagram we cannot really tell whether the tooth in question (allegedly a left lower premolar) was, in fact, a primate tooth. The original tooth was lost during the war. Leakey has claimed that because of the absence of a simian shelf (an important characteristic of the three existing large anthropoid apes), *Proconsul* is related to man. Finally, Lewis considers *Ramapithecus* and *Bramapithecus* as possible hominids (Hominidae?).

We rather question the correctness of Lewis' opinion, particularly about *Ramapithecus brevirostris*. *Ramapithecus* is known from the Chakrana upper jaw fragment with two molars, two premolars, a canine alveolus (socket), and a socket for the lateral incisor, and from the Kundal Nala lower jaw with two molars, two premolars, and a canine alveolus. The material was collected by the Yale-Cambridge India expedition led by Lewis in 1935. This species has the following characteristics:

1. Teeth almost smooth, with very few wrinklings in the enamel.
2. Small canines (inferred from size of alveoli) of diameter not larger than length of anterior premolar.

The original find was part of the Siwalik series from Harytalyangar in India. In his first account, Lewis (1937) argued that the find came from the Tatrot zone, close to the upper limit of the Pleistocene. More recently he has revised his view (Lewis and Pilbeam, 1965)—he now claims the fragment must have come from the Nagri strata—roughly corresponding to the upper Lower Pliocene—and that members of the team must have been mis-

FIG. 30. Teeth from upper jaw of *Ramapithecus brevirostris* from Harytalyangar, India. Note the striking resemblance to human teeth. Twice natural size. (After Simons.)

taken about the precise site. On an expedition to Pakistan, I myself discovered *Ramapithecus* remains in the *upper* Dhok-Pathan strata, and have accordingly decided that, in view of the marked faunistic differences obtained in the various Siwalik zones, the name "*Ramapithecus*" must be reserved for the original find, at least until such time as the material has been evaluated more fully.

Lewis and Pilbeam, for their part, have applied the name to a variety of forms, including particularly three species formerly classified as *Dryopithecus* (and/or *Bramapithecus*) from the Siwalik hills, but treat Lewis's *Ramapithecus,* cf., *longirostris* from Kunda Nala (Chinji zone), as a species of *Dryopithecus*. According to these authors, *Ramapithecus* also includes Leakey's *Kenya-pithecus* from the Upper Miocene of Fort Ternan (Kenya), of which we know little more than that it had small canines; and a lower jaw from the Lower Pleistocene of China, classified by Woo as *Dryopithecus*. Now, the location of these finds suggest that *Ramapithecus* must have enjoyed a highly improbable geographical distribution, more so since this form is also supposed to include one of the *Dryopithecus* teeth from the Swabian bean ore. This is an eroded upper molar with the same ridge between the two rear cusps (hypocone—metacone) as the well-preserved molar shown in figure 23, and undoubtedly belongs to the same species as the latter.

As if the confusion were not great enough, Leakey recently (1967) explained that his *Kenyapithecus* was no *Ramapithecus,* but that his *Sivapithecus* from the Lower Miocene of Kenya—which according to Simon and Pilbeam is a *Dryopithecus*—must be a *Kenyapithecus* which, incidentally, he considers a hominid. In short, the classification of *Kenyapithecus* seems to be extremely uncertain and will continue to be so until more conclusive finds are brought to light. In particular, it is impossible to decide at this stage whether or not *Ramapithecus* was a Tertiary ancestor of man.

Meanwhile, we must agree with Gregory that hominids and pongids have been derived from the *Dryopithecus* group. Hence Simpson is entitled to classify living pongids as Ponginae, and fossil pongids as Dryopithecinae, even though this classification cannot possibly reflect any natural distinction. We, for our part, decided not to follow Schlosser and Simpson in this respect. We consider that the hominoidea must have consisted of three groups. A neutral, completely extinct group, unlike any living species of anthropoid ape, derived from unspecialized forms. The anthropoid apes branched off from this group through overspecialization of canines and better adaptation to arboreal life, and the Hominidae branched off through reduction of the canines and by the assumption of an erect posture. We can only guess at the point in geological time when this division occurred. According to Osborn, it took place as early as the Oligocene, and according to Weinert (whose opinion is not shared by any other expert), man and the chimpanzee still had a common ancestor in the Upper Pliocene. We believe (with Gregory) that the separation may have taken place in the Upper Miocene or the Lower Pliocene—about 10,000,000 to 15,000,000 years ago. This interval strikes us as quite adequate, when we consider the rapid development of man in the Pleistocene—roughly 1,000,000 years ago.

In 1954, Hürzeler first suggested that in *Oreopithecus* we have "evidence of the existence of a Tertiary hominid."

> *Oreopithecus* Gervais, 1872. Medium size; small canines; molars of upper jaw with crista obliqua running close to the outer back cusp. Inner back cusp (hypoconus) with transverse crest. Lower jaw: first molar with original front inner cusp (paraconid), middle cusp (mesoconid) and very small central hypoconulid on the back edge. No Dryopithecus pattern. Last molar unusually long and with large hypoconulid. Front premolar bicuspid and smaller than its neighbor. Lower Plio-

cene. Numerous jaw fragments from ligniferous strata in Upper Italy (Mt. Bamboli, Casteani); Hürzeler recently discovered a nearly complete skeleton near Grosetto. The species probably occurs in Bessarabia.

As we see, *Oreopithecus bambolii* has been known for a very long time; we agree with Schwalbe (1915) and Schlosser that it is a representative of a distinct family. There is no doubt that particularly the molars of its lower jaw are very reminiscent of the Cercopithecines, and Simpson (1945) has, in fact, classified it as such, despite "certain peculiarities which make its position uncertain." As Gregory stated much earlier, *Oreopithecus* does not represent a morphological transition between the Cercopithecinae and the Pongidae.

FIG. 31. Right lower molar of man compared with that of *Oreopithecus*. Note the differences in dental pattern. Twice natural size. (After E. Selenka and J. Hürzeler.)

Hürzeler's view that *Oreopithecus* was a Tertiary hominid seems to be based too one-sidedly on its small canine and its generally bicuspid first lower premolar which Remane has shown to differ in structure from man's. We consider it crucial that the molars of *Oreopithecus* lack the *Dryopithecus* pattern characteristic of all anthropoid apes ever since the Miocene, and also of man (Fig. 31). Since, moreover, the crown pattern of *Oreopithecus* shows no traces whatsoever of a *Dryopithecus* pattern, we may take it that *Oreopithecus* represented a distinct branch of the main stem as early as the Miocene. In other words, it was a terminal form, probably with a characteristic predecessor in the Lower Tertiary.

Apidium Osborne, 1908. Lower jaw fragment only. Last premolar very simple. First premolar still with paraconid, and without crests between the cusps. Median cusp (hypoconulid) present. Last molar greatly elongated. Lower Oligocene of Egypt.

As Gregory has shown, we may tentatively look upon *Apidium phiomense* as a precursor of the Oreopithecidae. Since the same strata contained *Parapithecus* (primitive type with lemuroid characteristics), *Propliopithecus,* the precursor of the Pongids, and *Moeripithecus markgrafi,* the possible precursor of the Cercopithecines, the three groups of Old World Anthropoidea which we have distinguished must already have been distinct by the time the strata were laid down. While both the Cercopithecoidea and the Hominoidea still have living representatives, the Oreopithecoidea disappeared in the Lower Pliocene.

The Australopithecus Discoveries

In 1924, quarry workers in Taungs (Bechuanaland) came across a small skull in an ancient cave (Figs. 32 and 33). From its milk teeth, it appeared that the skull belonged to an immature individual. Because of its strange mixture of man and apelike characteristics, *Australopithecus africanus,* as Dart came to call it, proved extremely difficult to classify. Later, through the efforts particularly of Dr. Broom, further related fossils were dug up near Swartkrans, Sterkfontein, Kromdraai, Makapan, and other sites. In Makapan, Professor Dart came across charcoal fragments, from which he inferred that *Australopithecus* must have made fire. Hence he called the find *Australopithecus prometheus.* Broom, who wished to stress the manlike characteristics of his finds, called them *Paranthropus* and *Plesianthropus.*

Since then, a great many more *Australopithecus* teeth,

skulls, and jaw fragments have been dug up, but very little of the rest of the skeleton.

Below, we have arranged the *Australopithecus* finds, not in the chronological order of their discovery, but in

FIG. 32. Front view of original Taungs skull of *Australopithecus africanus*.

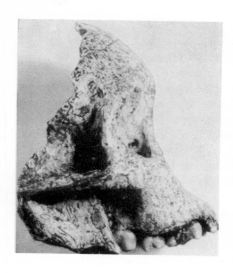

FIG. 33. Skull of *Australopithecus africanus*, seen from the side.

descending geological age. The original names are retained.

> *Australopithecus africanus* Dart, 1925, Taungs.
> One immature skull;
> *Plesianthropus transvaalensis* Broom, 1936, Sterk-
> fontein. Skull fragments; 141 teeth; a few bones
> including pelvis;
> *Australopithecus prometheus* Dart, 1947, Maka-
> pansgat. Skull fragments, 28 teeth, a few bones
> including pelvis;
> *Paranthropus crassidens* Broom, 1949, Swart-
> krans (richest site). Skull fragments (two skulls
> with sagittal crests), 273 permanent teeth and 38
> milk teeth; complete jaw;
> *Paranthropus robustus* Broom, 1938, Kromdraai.
> Few fragments; 17 permanent teeth; 6 milk teeth
> (milk teeth completely molarized in lower jaw).
> Material from some 70 individuals;
> *Zinjanthropus boisei* Leakey, East Africa. Near
> adult skull with sagittal crest. Cranial capacity c.
> 600 cc. Very coarse face; nostrils apelike, premo-
> lars and molars gigantic, canines and incisors dis-
> proportionally small. Lowest Middle Pleistocene
> (Layer I) of Olduvai, Tanganyika.—Two teeth
> from Layer II probably belong here (1958), and
> one lower jaw from Lake Natron (1964).

> In a recent monograph of the skull of *Zinjan-
> thropus,* Tobias has suggested that all the relevant
> fossils belong to the genus *Australopithecus,* com-
> prising the three species *A. africanus, A. robustus,*
> and *A. boisei.*

The classification of the australopithecines has been the
subject of much controversy. While Simpson (1945) still
included them among the pongids, there is no longer any
doubt that they were much closer to man than any anthropoid ape. Following Heberer, many authors distinguish
the australopithecines from true men, or Euhomini, by
calling them Praehomini. (The attempt of some anthropologists to alter their name to *Australanthropus* runs

counter to the established rules of nomenclature.) Unfortunately the name "Praehomini" suggests that this
group contains the real ancestors of the Euhomini, which,
as we shall see, is not the case.

In 1954, Robinson rearranged three genera containing
five species into two genera with one species and two subspecies each. Of these, the genus *Australopithecus* is said
to be distinguished from *Paranthropus* by its larger canines and slightly different milk teeth (Fig. 34). It appears, however, that these differences are not basic, but
due to the gradual molarization of the milk teeth (Fig.
35). By molarization we mean the process whereby the
front milk molars gradually change their crown pattern
until the morphological distinction between front and
back teeth disappears. This process is particularly striking in the permanent teeth of such modern Perissodactyla
(odd-toed mammals) as the horse, the tapir, and the rhinoceros, and in the milk teeth of the lower apes. Molarization is therefore a form of specialization—hence the Kromdraai *Australopithecus* with its completely molarized first
milk tooth must have been the most recent, and the Sterkfontein *Australopithecus* with its slightly modified milk

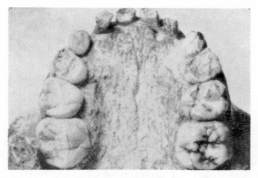

FIG. 34. *Australopithecus africanus:* upper milk teeth and first permanent molars. Slightly magnified.

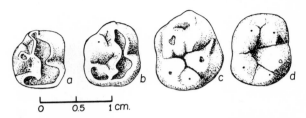

FIG. 35. The first lower milk molars of *Australopithecus* in increasing order of molarization. (a) Sterkfontein; (b) Taungs; (c) Swartkrans; (d) Kromdraai. (After J. T. Robinson.)

teeth, the oldest type. These paleontologico-morphological conclusions agree so completely with the stratigraphic results obtained from Professor Ewer's analysis of fossil carnivora that we must look on all known australopithecines as a single, fairly closed, group. In an early description of the milk teeth of *Australopithecus africanus*, Abel was able to show that these teeth were specialized in quite a different way from those of modern man: "The highly specialized teeth [of *Australopithecus*] have characteristics that can only be brought into a direct phylogenetic relationship with those of the hominids on the unlikely assumption that *Australopithecus* has partly gone back on its own evolution."

The australopithecines have closed rows of teeth with small canines in both the lower and the upper jaws. The molars are very much larger than those of modern man, but the incisors are disproportionally small (Fig. 36). The teeth show a marked inward reduction, which has influenced not only the shape of the incisors and canines, but even that of the premolars (Figs. 37–38). While the front premolar of *Australopithecus* is invariably smaller than the back premolar, the reverse is true of hominids in general and of modern man in particular. In anthropoid apes, the front premolar is, by the way, always the largest. In sharp contrast to the reduced front teeth, the chewing

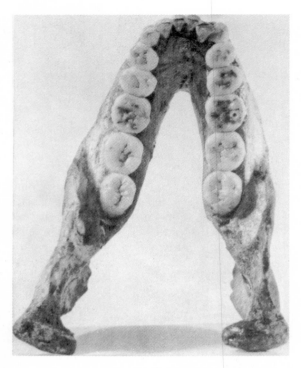

FIG. 36. Lower jaw of Swartkrans *Australopithecus,* slightly compressed. Note the large, coarse molars and disproportionately small canines and incisors. (Photogr.: R. Broom.)

teeth of australopithecines are large, and the back top and bottom molars are usually the most prominent—probably another result of specialization.

Though *Australopithecus* has fairly manlike teeth, its nostrils are still strikingly simian. The cranium is flat, the brow ridge is poorly developed. The cranial capacity must have been small; in *Plesianthropus* V it was found to be 482 cc., i.e., apelike. Though figures of up to 1,500 cc.

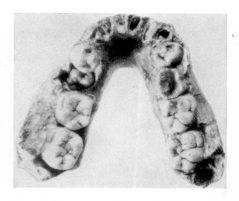

FIG. 37. Lower jaw of young Makapansgat *Australopithecus,* shedding its deciduous teeth. The molars have an external cingulum of the kind also found in species of *Pithecanthropus.* (Photogr.: R. A. Dart.)

may be found in the literature, they were wrongly calculated from estimates based on human characteristics. Two Swartkrans skulls even have a sagittal crest of the type only found in large anthropoid apes (Fig. 39). According to Robinson, the skulls in question were female, whereas sagittal crests are normally found on male anthropoid skulls only. In any case, the presence of the crest entitles us to assume a small brain capacity.

Zinjanthropus boisei Leakey (Zinji is an old African name for East Africa). Skull discovered July 17, 1959, by

FIG. 38. Upper canine of Swartkrans *Australopithecus.* Note the small crown and the large root. Natural size. (After J. T. Robinson.)

FIG. 39. Two original skulls of Swartkrans *Australopithecus* with sagittal crest. Left: a gorilla.

Mary Leakey 22 feet below the horizon separating Layers I and II of site FLK in the Olduvai Gorge, Tanganyika (results published in *Nature*, London, No. 4685). It is considered an australopithecine by all who have inspected the find. The skull has a sagittal crest similar to the Swartkrans skull (Fig. 40) and an estimated cranial

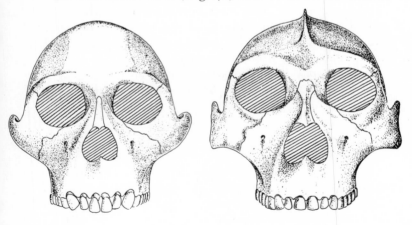

FIG. 40. Reconstruction of two *Australopithecus* skulls; left: Sterkfontein; right: Swartkrans. (After J. T. Robinson.)

capacity of 600 cc. It also has another crest, the *torus oc-cipitalis,* running right across the back of the skull. The skull is flattened and pulled downwards at the back. The mastoid process is broad, short, pointed, and well developed. The front of the relatively small skull—length c. 17.5 cm.—consists of an extremely coarse and elongated face. The brow ridge is fairly marked, the facial apertures are large, the skull bones are thin. The distance between the orbits is very great—about 32.5 mm. The nose is high up on the face, and the nostrils are more ape than manlike.

This skull goes with the largest set of teeth known in any man. The premolars and molars are no less than 72 mm. in length (mean length in modern man: 42.5 mm.). The second molar is the largest of the row; the surface of the third molar is somewhat smaller and so completely covered with irregular wrinkles that the original dental pattern is completely unrecognizable. This tooth resembles that of an orangutan much more closely than it does a human molar. Although all the teeth are strongly worn-down, the third molar is intact and projects from the row. (Among the Swartkrans finds, too, there were a number of strongly worn-down teeth with the third molar still in place.) By comparison, canines and incisors look small enough to have come from an altogether different jaw.

The same form also includes a gigantic and remarkably complete lower jaw discovered in 1964 near Lake Natron (about 20 miles from Olduvai). To judge by the associated fauna, it must have come from a stratum roughly corresponding to the upper part of Olduvai II. The ascending ramus is not particularly tall—that of the Olduvai skull must have been twice as tall as the Heidelberg—nor is the maxillary body. The canines and incisors are quite small and the remaining teeth are huge.

Tobias (1963) has compared the cranial capacities of all *Australopithecus* forms in which they can be determined accurately—seven in all—and has correlated the results with the known cranial capacities of anthropoid apes and *Pithecanthropus*. It would appear that, in this respect, the australopithecines were a long way off from *Pithecanthropus* or the *H. erectus* group.

Skull Capacity of Anthropoids, Australopithecines and Pithecanthropines (after Tobias)

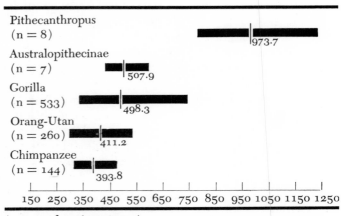

(*n = number of specimens*)

The australopithecines can easily be distinguished from the anthropoid apes by the near-human shape of their pelvis, from which we may take it that they walked on two feet. This assumption is supported by the position of their foramen magnum. We may summarize by saying that the australopithecines are far closer to man than they are to the anthropoid apes (Fig. 41). They constitute a distinct and fairly closed group of hominids, which must be considered a side branch of man's family tree, sharing a distant precursor with him.

A great difficulty arises from the claim that, since australopithecines made fire and tools, they must be considered full "men." We saw that Dart called his Makapan specimen *Australopithecus prometheus*, the fire-raiser, because of the charcoal near him. However, the mere discovery of pieces of charcoal does not entitle us to say that

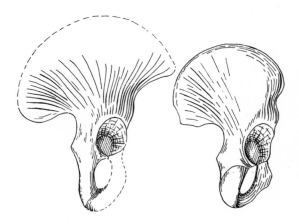

FIG. 41. Right hip bone of modern Bushman (right) and of Sterk-fontein *Australopithecus* (left). (After R. Broom.)

they were produced by men, for spontaneous bushfires are a far more likely explanation. Broom, probably one of the greatest experts on South African conditions, has rightly challenged Professor Dart's conclusion. He points out that, unlike Peking sites and many Neanderthal sites, *Australopithecus* sites have yielded no corroborative fragments of carbonized bones.

More equivocal still is the tool problem. No matter what the real explanation of the strange indentations on baboon skulls may be, they were certainly not caused in the way Dart has suggested. According to him, a number of evenly damaged humeri must have been used as percussion instruments, but we agree with Zapfe that the damage was more probably caused by hyenas. Since hyenas have been found in Makapan, and since the diagrams of Dart and Zapfe illustrating their different points of view are almost identical, the tool hypothesis can no longer be defended. Dart's further attempts to interpret other bone fragments as tools and his suggestion that the lower jaw of antelopes was used as a kind of saw, strike us as even more far-fetched. In this connection we must draw attention to the controversy about the Choukoutien bone fragments. From them Breuil inferred the existence of a "bone industry." According to his colleague Pei, with whom we agree, all the bones in question were broken accidentally or damaged by carnivores. Similarly, the alleged stone implements from Sterkfontein and Makapan are shown to be nothing of the sort by both their nature and their distribution. A recent find has come from strata containing Oldovan tools which, according to Leakey, were fashioned by *Zinjanthropus*. However, more recently a genuine hominid was discovered in the same complex.

Though the mammalian fauna associated with *Australopithecus* has not yet been fully investigated, remains of horses have been dug up at Swartkrans and Kromdraai. These two sites, at least, must have been of Pleistocene origin. In addition, a detailed comparison of carnivore remains has shown that Makapan and Taungs are the oldest sites, followed by Sterkfontein, Swartkrans, and Kromdraai, in that order. Not even the oldest, however, need be considered a Tertiary site. As we saw, the relative age of the sites can also be inferred from the morphology of the first lower milk teeth discovered in them.

Also from Swartkrans come the remains of *Telanthropus*, which, according to Broom and Robinson, is a true hominid. Its teeth are smaller than those of *Paranthropus crassidens* discovered in the same site. Since the site is relatively recent, we need not be surprised to learn that it holds true hominids alongside of australopithecines. Even so, it seems more likely that *Telanthropus* must be classified either as a particularly weak specimen of the typical *Paranthropus* or else as the representative of another *Australopithecus* group which stumbled across the site by accident.

Robinson believes that *Telanthropus* was a transitional form between the australopithecines and the existing hominids, and that Neanderthal forms are connected directly with *Telanthropus.* He concludes, therefore, that *Pithecanthropus* and *Sinanthropus* played no more than a very minor role in the history of mankind. This view, however, is plainly contradicted by the morphology of the last two.

In the Lower Pleistocene of East Africa, Kohl-Larssen came across an upper jaw fragment with two premolars, which Weinert has classified as *Meganthropus africanus,* i.e., as a relative of the Javanese *Meganthropus.* This classification strikes us as highly unlikely, for there is good reason why we should consider the jaw as belonging to a Central African australopithecine. Hence the australopithecines must have had a far wider distribution than was first believed.

The separate position of the australopithecines (Fig. 42) among the other hominids with which they share their posture and other characteristics has a parallel in the classification of another group of animals—the modern elephants. If we ignore the Sumatran elephant (which is probably only a subspecies of the Indian), we find two geographically distinct species: the Indian and the Afri-

FIG. 42. Reconstruction of an *Australopithecus,* drawn by W. Wandel.

can. Linnaeus originally included both in the genus
Elephas. They resemble each other in many respects:
both are similar in size, and both have similar tusks and
trunks. However, the ears of the Indian elephant are
smaller than those of the African.

Falconer's detailed investigation of their skeletons and
above all of their teeth has, however, shown that the two
types represent different evolutionary stages, and hence
different genera (or subgenera), viz. *Loxodonta africana*
and *Euelephas indicus*. *Loxodonta* has shorter teeth with
fewer ridges (maximum about twelve as against 24 in the
last upper and up to 27 in the lower molar of the Indian
elephant). The Indian type is therefore more highly specialized. Despite their different evolutionary rate, both
have a common ancestor in the primitive *Archidiskodon*
of the Lowest Pleistocene. Hence an interval of only
("only" in the geological sense) some 2,000,000 years was
enough for two like yet systematically distinct types to
develop. A similar interval must also have covered the
separate phylogenetic emergence of the most recent
known australopithecines and the *Pithecanthropus* group
from their common ancestor in the Pliocene.

The Homo Habilis Discoveries

Under the name of *Homo habilis* (*habilis* meaning skill-
ful), Leakey, Tobias, and Napier (1964) have combined
a whole series of human fossils from Olduvai I and II
(Fig. 43).

The lower jaws brought up from these two beds are
morphologically so different that, in my view, they must
be treated as two distinct forms, more so since the chronological gap between the two beds is exceedingly great—
some 600,000 years! Although no detailed description has
appeared so far, controversy about the correct classification of these finds is already in full spate.

The best preserved fragments from Bed I are an incomplete skull and a broken but otherwise well-preserved lower jaw. The skull (Olduvai 7) is considered typical of the new species and consists of two incomplete parietal bones.

FIG. 43. Lower jaw of *Homo habilis* from Olduvai I, East Africa. The relative dimensions of the canines and incisors make it probable that this jaw belonged to precursor of man. (After Tobias.)

According to very careful estimates by Tobias (1964), the cranial capacity was 642–723 cc, i.e., greater than that of *Australopithecus* but smaller than that of *Pithecanthropus*. From the same individual, we also have a lower jaw, an upper molar, a clavicle and part of a hand. The lower jaw, with the last tooth on the left and the last two teeth on the right missing, has large molars and sharply defined premolars, together with remarkably even canines and incisors. Robinson does not accept Tobias's criteria, and treats *Homo habilis* as an australopithecine, but I believe that despite the greater variability of the latter, the find should be treated as a hominine.

The most important find from Bed 2 (Olduvai 13) consists of the remains of a relatively small skull, fragments of the upper jaw, and a complete set of lower jaw teeth. As we were able to show (Tobias and von Koenigswald, 1964), the teeth correspond so closely with those of *Pithecanthropus modjokertensis* of Java that both must have attained the same level of evolution. And just as "*Habilis* II" is older than *Pithecanthropus erectus,* so *H. erectus* of Java corresponds to a (younger) *Pithecanthropus* from the upper part of Olduvai II, which has not yet been named and to which we shall come back in the next section. Campbell (1965) has accordingly distinguished between "*Homo erectus habilis*" and "*Homo erectus modjokertensis.*"

One of the oldest human remains, which must provisionally be included here, consists of the fragment of an upper arm discovered in Kanopoi, on Lake Rudolph, Northern Kenya by B. Patterson (1965) of Harvard University. Potassium-argon dating methods have shown that the fragment is 2.5 million years old, and a computer analysis has suggested that the find is morphologically closer to *Homo* than it is to *Australopithecus.*

A further find, which must possibly be included here as well, was made by Y. Coppens (1960) in the vicinity of Lake Chad. It has been called *Tchadanthropus uxorius,* and consists of a much-eroded anterior portion of a skull with a lofty frontal bone; no teeth were present. The brow ridges were probably reduced by erosion.

In short, therefore, and as was only to be expected, a stage more primitive still than *Pithecanthropus* seems to be emerging from obscurity.

The Homo Erectus Discoveries

This section includes the *Pithecanthropus* group, so called after *Pithecanthropus erectus,* the first to be discovered. We have just pointed out that it is impossible to tell precisely when this group first emerged, nor can we say with any certainty just where it ends. Thus the Solo skulls of Java have been variously classified as *erectus* and as *sapiens* (i.e., as Neanderthal man).

THE PITHECANTHROPUS DISCOVERIES

By *Pithecanthropus* we refer to human fossils from the Lowest and Lower Pleistocene (up to about the beginning of the great Mindel-Riss interglacial). They represent the oldest human remains known, since, despite promising reports, the Tertiary has not yet produced fossils with any bearing on the evolution of modern man. We begin with a few Javanese finds.

The Javanese discoveries

Trinil Fauna: *Pithecanthropus erectus* D.
Djetis Fauna: *Pithecanthropus dubius* v. K.
      Pithecanthropus modjokertensis v. K.
      Meganthropus palaeojavanicus v. K.

The Djetis and Trinil fauna of Java is composed very much like that of the Pinjor and Narbada layers in India. Both are separated by the so-called "Boulder Conglomerate," which, according to De Terra, was produced during the second (Mindel) glaciation and continues as far as the Himalayas. In other words, the upper limit of the Djetis layers would roughly correspond to the beginning of the Mindel glaciation, while the Trinil layers correspond to the beginning of the "great" interglacial.

> *Meganthropus palaeojavanicus* v. K., 1941. The first find was a lower jaw fragment with three teeth (two premolars, one molar) and the alveolus of a small canine. Traces of a typically human *spina mentalis*. After the war, another jaw of equal size was found. It was deformed in the chin region and lacked teeth except for a displaced last molar. Both finds at Sangiran.

Meganthropus had the largest human lower jaw (Fig. 44) so far discovered. It was roughly the size of a gorilla's

FIG. 44. External view of lower jaw fragment of *Meganthropus paleojavanicus* from the Lower Pleistocene of Sangiran (Central Java). Natural size.

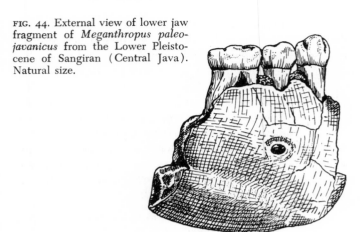

(length of first molar: Meganthropus 14.5 mm.; gorilla 15.5 mm.; average *Homo sapiens* 11.1 mm.). Robinson, who considers the jaw as that of *Paranthropus*, has shown that the two are comparable in size and structure. Since the hominids and the australopithecines certainly go back to a common form, the earliest differentiated types must have resembled one another. Hence what small differences there are assume a paramount importance. Now, *Meganthropus* has a prominent first molar, just like all older hominids and even a few races of modern man (Eskimos, Melanesians), while the first premolar of the australopithecines is smaller than the second. Again, the second premolar of *Meganthropus* has only one root, like that of man, while those of the australopithecines have the double roots of anthropoid apes. The discovery of further material is bound to reveal still further differences. In any case, all the experts agree that *Meganthropus* is a very important primitive type.

A recent reconstruction (1966) of one of the three extant lower jaws has shown that the frontal section must have been very much narrower, and the canines and incisors very much smaller than was originally assumed.

The jaw, in particular, bears a striking resemblance to that of an *Australopithecus,* but whether it actually belonged to one—which would introduce not only considerable phylogenetic but also great zoological complications —has not yet been established. In particular, certain features of the teeth suggest that their owner must have been more "human" than any of the South African forms.

Little can be said about the next find, *Pithecanthropus dubius,* reconstructed from the fragment of a tall and slender lower jaw. Its dental pattern and symphysial section differ so greatly from those of *Meganthropus* that we must consider it a special type.

> *Pithecanthropus dubius* v. K., 1948. Based on a small jaw fragment discovered in Sangiran (1939). The jaw itself was large, but more slender than that of *Meganthropus* and with a divergent symphysis. Dental pattern of molars very complicated. Weidenreich at first assumed that the jaw was that of an orangutan (hence the name *dubius*); however the alveolus of the canine is too small and manlike for an ape.

Much more is known about the third type discovered in the Djetis layer, viz. *Pithecanthropus modjokertensis.*

> *Pithecanthropus modjokertensis* v. K., 1936. The first find, a child's skull only 14 cm. long, was made near Modjokerto (East Java). Originally described as *Homo.* Later, the following were discovered at Sangiran: a lower jaw (Fig. 45, 1936), first classified as *Pithecanthropus erectus,* and then (1938–39) fragments of a skull with a well-preserved upper jaw and also numerous individual teeth.

The lower and upper jaw together make up the most primitive dentition of any known man. As in most anthropoids, the largest lower molar is the last, and the largest upper molar is the second (in modern man, the largest molar in either jaw is the first). The top first premolar has

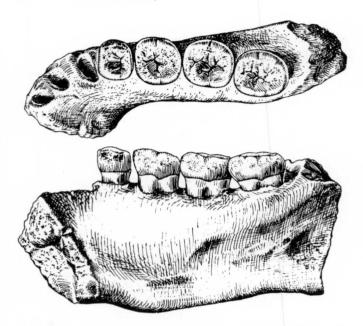

FIG. 45. Upper and external views of lower jaw fragment of *Pithecanthropus modjokertensis* from the L. Pleistocene of Sangiran (Central Java). Natural size.

retained its original three roots; the upper canine is not horizontal and, though worn down front and back, still projects above the chewing area. From the diastema, corresponding to the "monkey gap," we can tell that the canine must have been well above 1 cm. in height. The teeth, from the last molar to the canine, lie in a straight row, and both rows of teeth are bent slightly toward the front. The molars are separated from the incisor arch by the diastema, which is not found in the continuous dental arch of modern man (Fig. 46).

The dentition of *P. modjokertensis* not only differs from that of modern (and fossil) man, but also from *Australopithecus*. On the other hand, the narrow nose of *Pithecan-*

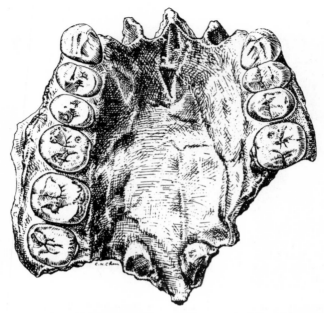

FIG. 46. Upper jaw of *Pithecanthropus modjokertensis.* Note the
(natural) size of the teeth and the shape of the dental arch. The
incisors have fallen out; they were separated from the canines by a
clear gap. For a reconstruction of this jaw, cf. Fig. 79.

thropus is completely human, while that of australopithecines is identical with the chimpanzees'.

From their structure, clearly emphasized by the gap,
we may infer that the canines of man's direct precursor
had a greater functional importance than the other teeth.
Much has been written, and still more surmised, on the
subject of human canines. It has often been suggested
that, since they are also found in *Parapithecus,* small canines are a primitive characteristic of man. While *Parapithecus* did, in fact, have a small unspecialized canine,
he also had unspecialized premolars which certainly bear
no comparison with man's. Remane has argued most con-

FIG. 47. Reconstruction of the skull of *Pithecanthropus modjokertensis* from Sangiran, Central Java. Part of forehead and rear part of lower jaw have been added. The cranial capacity was a mere 750 cc.

vincingly that the overhang of the front lower human milk molar can only be explained as an adaptation to what must have been a larger canine. Weidenreich has shown how disproportionately large the root of Peking man's canine was in relation to the crown. These two views are fully borne out by the Javanese jaw (Fig. 47). Earlier types with small or reduced canines, e.g., the australopithecines or *Oreopithecus* must therefore be excluded from the list of our direct, and possibly even our indirect, precursors.

This skull, too, has been reconstructed afresh, but on the basis of the original fragments by Dr. P. G. Wandel. The reconstruction showed that the skull must have been slightly shorter and, above all, that it must have had a considerably smaller capacity, which we have estimated at 750 cc. Since the robustness of the skull and of the teeth suggests that the owner was a male, it is reasonable to assume that females must have had a cranial capacity of only 600–650 cc. In other words, the cranial capacity was only slightly above that of anthropomorphic forms, and this accords with the primitive nature of the teeth. An incisor belonging to the skull in figure 47 was spatular, i.e., it had a protruding rim.

The presence of different human types in one and the same complex of Javanese layers reflects the mixed character of the mammalian fauna in general. In the Tertiary, the great Sunda group was still a series of smaller islands which subsequently grew and joined together. At times they formed a more or less contiguous land mass, particularly during the Ice Age when the sea level of the entire world was some 100–160 feet lower than it is today. While the sea bed drops steeply away west of Sumatra, south of Java, and east of Borneo, it is no more than some 160 feet below sea level between the islands themselves.

The oldest fauna to reach Java was of Indian origin and corresponds to the known fauna of the Himalayan foothills. The main representatives were primitive elephants, and quite particularly hippopotami of the genus *Hexaprotodon* (with six incisors instead of the four found in the existing *Tetraprotodon*). This ancient fauna is called Siva-Malayan and preceded the Sino-Malayan, which contains many types now extinct in China but characteristic of modern Malaya. Examples are: the orangutan, various gibbons, the tapir, and the Malayan bear. From the Javanese finds we may conclude that both the Indian and the Chinese fauna contained distinct types of early man, and that the two met in Java.

Only one type of man is known from the more recent Trinil layers of Java: *Pithecanthropus* or *Homo erectus* (Fig. 48).

> *Pithecanthropus erectus* Dubois, 1894. Dubois' classical discoveries at Trinil consisted of a skull top (1891) and a femur resembling that of modern man (1892). Further femur fragments were subsequently found in Dubois' collection. From

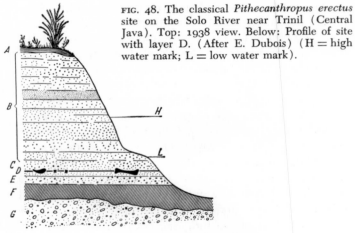

FIG. 48. The classical *Pithecanthropus erectus* site on the Solo River near Trinil (Central Java). Top: 1938 view. Below: Profile of site with layer D. (After E. Dubois) (H = high water mark; L = low water mark).

the temporal region of a second Sangiran skull (von Koenigswald, 1937–Fig. 49) paleontologists were able to classify this disputed species as a hominid. Cranial capacity 775 cc. Another skull fragment (an almost square parietal) of an immature individual was also discovered at Sangiran (1938), together with isolated teeth. The premolars were small and resembled those of the Heidelberg jaw.

From the primitive form of his skull top and femur, Dubois inferred that they were of Tertiary origin, even though the character of the accompanying fauna belied this view. It was only in 1934, when the sequence of Pleistocene layers of Java was better understood, that it became clear that *P. erectus* must have lived in the Middle Pleistocene.

The name *Pithecanthropus,* originally coined by Haeckel and later applied to a hypothetical link between the apes and man, was deliberately adopted by Dubois who believed he had actually found that link. At first, he thought the creature resembled a chimpanzee, but in 1894 he changed his mind and published his classical *"Pithe-*

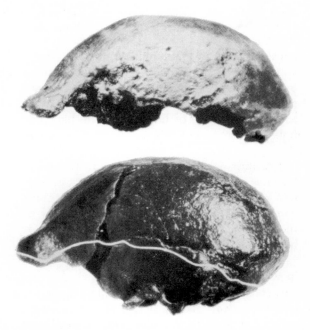

FIG. 49. Skull of *Pithecanthropus erectus*. Top: Trinil skull, 1892; Bottom: Skull II of Sangiran, 1937. The white line marks the lower edge of the first find.

canthropus erectus, a manlike transitional form from
Java." Since, lacking the more conclusive temporal region,
Dubois based his views on the skull top alone, many students were rather skeptical. In fact, there is no other find
on which more controversial literature has been published.

Only after the discovery of Peking men did the controversy subside. Oddly enough, Dubois, who had over-
loaded his own finds with far too much theory, never ad-
mitted the relationship between *Pithecanthropus* and
Sinanthropus. He described the latter as a degenerate
Neanderthal man and quite unexpectedly turned his own
find into a giant gibbon. The second skull from Sangiran
was dismissed by him as a fraud. When Dubois died in
1940, at the age of 82 years, he had not bothered to examine the 1937 finds.

Pithecanthropus I and II agree even in what might be
considered purely individual traits, e.g., the sharp back-
ward slope of the frontal region above and behind the
orbits. Moreover, *Pithecanthropus* II (Fig. 50) showed—
as Weinert had suggested earlier—that Dubois, misled by
a projecting piece of bone fragment, had placed the ear
holes too high, and had therefore misconstructed a low
skull.

The 1937 skull is very thick (1 cm. average), and therefore has a capacity of no more than 775 cc.—less than half
that of a modern European. Cranial casts show that the
convolutions of the brain were more sharply defined than
those of modern man; in the frontal region they resembled those of the chimpanzee.

The first skull had heavy brow ridges, and the second,
in which this part of the skull was damaged, must have
had considerably smaller ones. The ear region, and especially the deep groove in the temporal bone, which receives the condyle of the jaw, was typically manlike. On
the other hand, the mastoid process behind the ear was
rudimentary and far more reminiscent of anthropoid apes

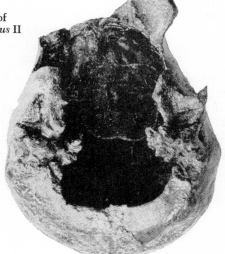

FIG. 50. Front and bottom view of skull of *Pithecanthropus erectus* II of Sangiran.

than of man. Since, however, the first skull had a well-developed mastoid process, the second may possibly represent an individual deviation.

A further *erectus* skull (III) was also discovered in Sangiran (1963) but unfortunately the frontal area was missing. This skull proved to be slightly more elongated than No. II; Teuku Jacob has estimated its capacity at 975 cc. This would seem to prove that skulls I and II came from females, and that the cranial capacity of *H. erectus* must have varied between 775 and 975 cc. depending on sex.

Unlike the Djetis layers, the Trinil layers have yielded few good jaws. Dubois found a small fragment of a toothless lower jaw near Trinil as early as 1890. It was considerably lower and more slender than the jaws we have just described and probably belonged to *Pithecanthropus erectus* (Fig. 51). In Trinil, Dubois also discovered a front lower premolar of small dimensions (the two large upper molars of Trinil, classified by Dubois as *Pithecanthropus,* must have belonged to an orangutan). The author came across a similar premolar in Sangiran, together with some upper teeth. These finds prove that the teeth of *Pithecanthropus erectus* were comparable in size with those of modern man. Hence it is possible that the jaw of the Heidelberg man (which we shall be discussing at greater length) was rightly attributed to the *Pithecanthropus* group (Fig. 52).

All the Javanese finds were alluvial river and sea deposits. On the other hand, the Chinese *Sinanthropus* must

FIG. 51. Rear view of skull of *Pithecanthropus erectus* II of Sangiran.

FIG. 52. Reconstruction of a *Pithecanthropus,* drawn by W. Wandel.

himself have lived on the site where his fossils were found. As a result, we have a greater concentration of fossils, but lack any kind of stratigraphical knowledge about them. The Chinese finds probably go back to the end of the Mindel glaciation.

In China, fossil remains are sold as dragons' teeth and dragons' bones by pharmacists who collect them for their "remedial" properties. Among a collection of such fossils, acquired by Heberer in Peking during the Boxer rebellion, Schlosser discovered a human tooth. Ever since, students have been convinced that the neighborhood of Peking must be studded with fossils. As early as 1918, G. Anderson discovered a rich mammalian site at Choukoutien, some 30 miles from Peking, and, in 1921 and again in 1923, Zdansky supervised excavations there on behalf of the Swedish Academy. While preparing his material in Upsala, he discovered two human teeth which he classified as belonging to *Homo* sp. Meanwhile the site had aroused the interest of the Canadian anatomist Davidson Black who, with the help of the Rockefeller Foundation, carried out large-scale excavations. On October 16, 1927, Dr. Bohlin discovered an unusually large and highly wrinkled first lower molar, which Davidson Black immediately took for that of a previously unknown type of man: *Sinanthropus pekinensis*.

> *Sinanthropus pekinensis* Davidson Black, 1927.
> Isolated teeth, 1927; first skull, 1928. Early material: fragments of 14 skulls and 14 lower jaws with 148 teeth; remarkably little of the rest of the skeleton. Material lost during World War II (1941). Postwar finds consist of only a few teeth and one lower jaw (Newspaper report).
>
> Isolated teeth of *Sinanthropus* were found among dragons' teeth in pharmacies in Canton and Hong Kong. This material originated from unknown sites in Southern China (Kwangsi and Kwangtung provinces).

Further finds showed that Black had been right to consider the controversial find a new type of man. From the 1928 skull he was able to prove further that *Sinanthropus* must have been a relative of the Javanese *Pithecanthropus* (Fig. 53). Unfortunately, Dubois did not accept Black's conclusions and continued to look upon *Sinanthropus* as a degenerate Neanderthal man. All further scientific discussions with him foundered on his obstinacy.

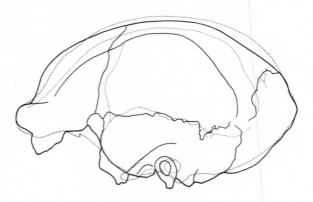

FIG. 53. Superimposed braincases of *Sinanthropus* (continuous line) and of *Pithecanthropus erectus* (dotted line). (After F. Weidenreich.)

The Choukoutien site lies in a strategic position, just where the western mountain chain borders the plain of Petchili. The site is a narrow gorge, partially collapsed, and partially filled with rubble. It must have originally been more than 160 feet deep. Here *Sinanthropus* camped under projecting rocks and in small caves, and here he left the remains of his prey. From layers of ash we can tell that he made fire. He also fashioned stone tools, unfortunately of quartz, a material singularly unsuited to the purpose. As a result, we cannot compare the stone industry of Choukoutien with any other. The remains of his prey consisted mainly of deer and boar, and to a lesser extent of horses, buffalo, and rhinoceros. The bones of countless carnivores, above all of hyenas, indicate that man's place was either challenged by these animals or else taken over when he moved on.

The most interesting prey, however, was man himself. Damaged human bones leave no doubt that Peking man was both a cannibal and a head-hunter. Cannibalism may be inferred from the few, but completely broken, femurs which were cracked open to extract the marrow; head-hunting from the fact that wherever the fragments of the 14 skulls found allowed a complete reconstruction, the foramen magnum was invariably widened. This was the habit of head-hunters, who extracted the brains of their victims and ate them for their miraculous powers. What with broken skulls and bones, very little indeed is known of the skeletons of more than 50 individuals, buried in a layer more than 160 feet thick.

A peculiarity of Peking man was his marked sexual dimorphism. The lower jaws of males and females differ so much in size (cf. Fig. 82) that they were originally attributed to two different species. A closer investigation has, however, made it clear that the differences merely show that the females were more graceful than the males. Marked sexual dimorphism is also found in the large anthropoid apes, particularly in the gorilla.

The skull of *Sinanthropus* bears a striking resemblance to that of *Pithecanthropus,* except that the forehead is somewhat steeper, and hence the brow ridge protrudes more strongly from the face (Fig. 54). This skull, too, is widest in the temporal region, quite unlike that of the more recent types. The brain capacity fluctuates from 915 cc. in a young to 1,015 cc. in an adult female, and to 1,225 cc. in an adult male. As in *Pithecanthropus,* the skull bones are very thick, and the groove holding the condyle of the lower jaw is deep.

Weidenreich has described the teeth of Peking man in a detailed paper. They were far coarser and more numerous than those of modern man; their pulp cavity was exceptionally deep (taurodont), and, most striking of all, the upper canine was unusually strong and pointed, while the lower was spatular like ours. The roots of the canines were powerful, and suggest that the precursor of Peking man must have had even larger canines which underwent a marked reduction first at the crown and later at the

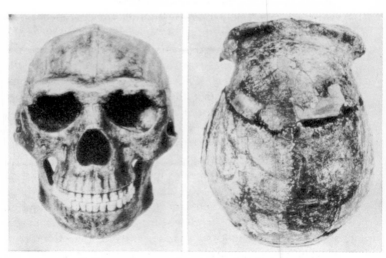

FIG. 54. *Sinanthropus pekinensis.* Top view of skull (right); reconstructed front view of whole skull (left). (After F. Weidenreich.)

roots. In association with the large canines, the lower premolars, too, were exceptionally large (the mean height of
the front premolar is greater than the maximum of modern
Europeans). In addition, the front premolar was longer
than the one behind it. This is a primitive characteristic of
anthropoid apes and of the oldest types of man, including
a few existing races (e.g., the Greenland Eskimos). In
modern Europeans, the proportions are usually the other
way round and the differences smaller—certainly much
smaller than in *Australopithecus* (see charts).

All we know of the milk teeth of *Sinanthropus* is based
on a few lower jaw fragments. The primitive cusp and
ridge formation is still found in the corresponding tooth
of modern Malayans and is therefore no special characteristic of early man. In any case, the dental arch of *Sinanthropus* is far more human than that of *Pithecanthropus
modjokertensis*.

Length of the two lower premolars

	Mean Value (*in mm.*)	Minima-Maxima (*in mm.*)
Front Premolar (P₃)		
Sinanthropus		
(Lower Jaw G)	9.1	7.8–9.8
Modern Man:		
Australian aborigine		6.6–8.5
Melanesian	6.7	6.5–7.6
European		5.2–8.1
Back Premolar (P₄)		
Sinanthropus		
(Lower Jaw G)	8.5	8.2–9.8
Modern Man:		
Australian aborigine		6.9–8.2
Melanesian	6.9	6.5–8.0
European		5.2–9.0

Measurements of some Pithecanthropus skulls

	Maximum length	Maximum breadth	Cephalic index	Distance from basion to bregma	Cranial capacity (in cc.)
Pithecanthropus I	183(e) (153)	135	—	105(e)	935
Pithecanthropus II	176 (148)	129	76.5	105	775
Sinanthropus III	188 (156)	141	72.3	—	915
Sinanthropus XI	192 (167)	143	72.4	115(e)	1,015
Sinanthropus X	195.5 (173)	147	71.0	—	1,225

After Weidenreich (1943)   [*(e) = estimate*]

The figures in parentheses refer to the maximum length of the interior of the skull; the differences from outside lengths are considerable because of the thickness of the bones. The brain capacity is small.

Because of the close relationship between *Pithecanthropus* and *Sinanthropus,* some students have changed the name of *Sinanthropus* to *Pithecanthropus erectus pekinensis.* We have retained the old name, since the Javanese finds have not yielded sufficient comparative material to justify the change, and since some clear differences have not yet been adequately explained. Judging by the teeth alone, we must certainly consider *Pithecanthropus modjokertensis* as more primitive, and *Pithecanthropus erectus* as more highly evolved than *Sinanthropus.*

Although no important finds have been made in Choukoutien since World War II, Professor Woo has discovered a new site and a new type of man in China.

> *Sinanthropus lantianensis,* so called after the Lantian site in Shensi Province. Lower jaw (1963); skull-cap and upper-jaw fragment (1964). Morphologically and faunistically older than classical *Sinanthropus* (Fig. 55).

The lower jaw, which is massive, chinless, and has worn teeth, must have lacked rear molars on either side. It is the only jaw of this kind attributed to fossil man—the tendency to suppress "wisdom teeth" is more typical of his modern descendants.

A reconstruction suggests that the brow ridges must have been prominent. The cranial capacity was relatively

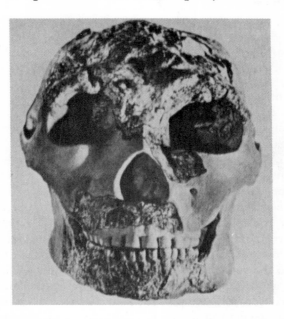

FIG. 55. Reconstruction of the skull of Lantian man from China. This skull is more primitive and older than that of classical Peking man. (After Woo.)

small (780 cc.) and hence close to that of *H. modjokerten-sis*, which it resembles in external appearance and to which it must have been in close chronological correspondence. No tools were found at the site, said to be of lower Middle Pleistocene origin.

Among the isolated teeth from Kwangsi and Kwang-tung sold by the Chinese pharmacies was a very large front premolar of *Sinanthropus*. Two of the upper molars have a special "Carabelli cusp," which, though common in man, is usually absent in Peking man. The definite evaluation of this "modern" trait will have to await the discovery of further material.

We must now return to Olduvai, and, in particular, to Leakey's find of a fine skull, which undoubtedly fits into the present scheme.

> *Pithecanthropus* sp. ("Homo erectus leakeyi").
> A fairly complete skull-cap without face or teeth and with enormous brow-ridges. The skull is elongated (20.9 cm.) and the occiput sharply cut off. No full scientific account has yet appeared.

The age of the bed has been given as 490,000, which would correspond to the Upper Trinil of Java. Hand axes in this layer suggest an early Chellean (Stage III) culture, which does not occur in Java.

The interpretation of this find, as well as of other remains, promises to make an interesting contribution to the history of African fossil man.

Telanthropus capensis from a cave deposit in Sterkfontein, South Africa, about which only very fragmentary information is available, is treated by some authorities as *Australopithecus* and by others as *H. erectus*.

To the *Pithecanthropus* group we should here like to add a few types known mainly by their lower jaws, and hence not fully comparable with the classical types reconstructed from jaws *and* skulls. Even so, there is no doubt that all are interrelated, and hence that *Pithecanthropus* must have lived in other parts of the world.

Palaeanthropus heidelbergensis Schoetensack, 1908. In 1907, a human lower jaw was discovered 75 feet below the surface of a sandpit at Mauer near Heidelberg. It was surrounded by the remains of an ancient elephant and of an Etruscan rhinoceros. The find represents the oldest human skeleton found in Europe, and probably goes back to a short, warm, interstadial of the Mindel glacial.

The jaw (Fig. 56) has remained the only human fragment dug up from the sands of Mauer during 70 years of intensive research. Schoetensack, who appreciated the importance of the site from the start, had to wait 20 years before even this fragment came to light!

Being a modest man, Schoetensack described the jaw as that of *Homo heidelbergensis*. One year later, Ameghino renamed it *Pseudhomo,* and since then it has been called a host of different names—last of all *Europanthropus*. Here we have referred to it as *Palaeanthropus,* a name coined by Bonarelli in 1909 to stress its differences in geological age and in size from *Homo* proper. Werth (1928) seems to have been the first to have classified the

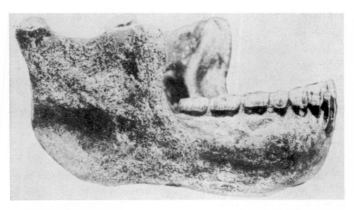

FIG. 56. The oldest find in Europe: side view of lower jaw of *Paleanthropus heidelbergensis* from Mauer, near Heidelberg. (After Schoetensack.)

Heidelberg find as *Pithecanthropus.* The first lower premolar of *Pithecanthropus erectus* (which is smaller than
that of *Sinanthropus*) corresponds fairly well in size with
that of the Heidelberg jaw (which, as we shall see, is
more massive than the typical Neanderthal jaw).

The well-preserved jaw (a few left teeth were stuck in
a concretion but were otherwise unimpaired) contains a
set of teeth that are quite modern except for their deep
pulp cavity (taurodontism). The jaw itself is chinless,
very large, and its ascending ramus is very broad and
squat. Such jaws are normally associated with a far more
primitive set of teeth. The dental arch is rounded; the
incisors, canines, and premolars are small and well pro-
portioned. The last molar is shorter than the second.

The new African finds, too, consist mainly of lower
jaws. The most important of all was made in 1955:

> *Atlanthropus mauritanicus* Arambourg, 1954.
> Discovered near Ternifine, Southern Algeria.
> Three lower jaws (I–III); a number of isolated
> teeth; a parietal bone (IV). Jaws and teeth are
> very powerful. The associated fauna seems to go
> back to the beginning of the Middle Pleistocene.

Jaw III (Fig. 57), in which most teeth are present and
whose rami are unimpaired, is probably the largest of all
fossilized lower jaws so far discovered—with the probable
exception of the poorly preserved jaw of *Meganthropus.*
It is certainly larger than the Heidelberg jaw and the
large lower jaw (GI) of Choukoutien.

Molars, premolars, and canine lie in a straight line; the
last molar is already slightly reduced; the canine is large,
but worn-down horizontally like a typical human tooth.
On its outer side, the jaw has a number of foramina: three
on the left, and two on the right side. *Sinanthropus* and
Pithecanthropus modjokertensis have up to five such
openings, but *Atlanthropus* I and II (Fig. 58) have only
one. The length of the three molars is: *Atlanthropus* III—
37 mm.; *Atlanthropus* I—39 mm.; and *Atlanthropus* II—42

FIG. 57. Side view of lower jaw of *Atlanthropus* III from Ternifine (Algeria). (After Arambourg.)

mm. The corresponding values in *Palaeanthropus* and *Sinanthropus* are 36.5 mm. and 38 mm. respectively.

Of the skull, only an isolated parietal fragment is known (*Atlanthropus* IV). In thickness, square shape, and nature of the arterial grooves it resembles the parietals of *Sinanthropus* and *Pithecanthropus erectus* III (1938).

Lower jaws of the Pithecanthropus group

	Maximum length	Maximum width (outer edge of condyles)	Height of symphysis	Height below first molar	Height of ascending ramus	Width of ascending ramus
Heidelberg	120	132.7	34	32	71	52
Sinanthropus (GI)	103	150	40	34	74	40
Atlanthropus II	110	—	35	34	72	45
Atlanthropus III	129	158	39	38	93	48

After Arambourg (1956)

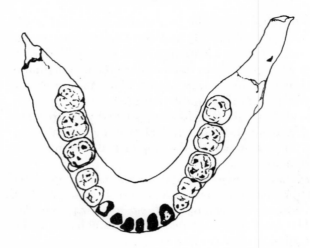

FIG. 58. Top view of lower jaw of *Atlanthropus* II. (After Arambourg.)

According to Cabot-Briggs, the *Pithecanthropus* group also includes the incomplete lower jaw from Rabat, Morocco (Marcais, 1934), whose three large lower molars—length of row: 37 mm.—have a basal cingulum like those of *Sinanthropus* but unlike those of Neanderthal man.

To sum up, the various *Pithecanthropus* forms, found in a continuous sequence of beds in both Sangiran and Olduvai, can be divided up as follows:

Pithecanthropus forms of comparable levels of development

China	Java (Sangiran)	East Africa (Olduvai)
(more recent form):	*erectus*	*erectus*
erectus pekinensis	*erectus*	("*leakeyi*")
(Older form):	*erectus*	*erectus*
erectus lantianensis	*modjokertensis*	("*habilis II*")

Thus the Trinil layers of Java would correspond to the upper part of Olduvai II, and the Djetis layers to the lower part—to what extent they also include Bed I, or perhaps even go deeper—the bottom layer in Sangiran is contiguous with the marine Upper Pliocene—has still to be determined by absolute dating methods.

All in all, it would therefore appear that primitive man enjoyed a wide distribution, and that he probably inhabited the major part of the tropics and sub-tropics of the Old World.

As we have shown at length in the last chapter, the australopithecines of Africa are a branch which split off from the main line leading to *Homo sapiens* in the Pliocene. The most important distinctions established so far may be summarized as follows:

Differences in skull structure and dentition

Australopithecus group	*Pithecanthropus group*
Skull bones thin	Skull bones thick
Nasal aperture chimpanzee-like	Nasal aperture human
Brow ridges (generally) weak	Brow ridges pronounced
Second upper molar invariably larger than first	Second upper molar smaller than first (except in the oldest types).
Lower back premolar with two roots	Lower back premolar with one root
Evolutionary tendencies	
Size of brain (probably) increasing	Size of brain strongly increasing
Most recent types (Swartkrans, Olduvai) with median crest.	Even oldest forms (presumably) without median crest.
Marked increase in size of molars and premolars.	Reduction in size of molars and premolars
Canines and incisors considerably reduced	Canines and incisors less markedly reduced
Milk teeth molarized	Milk teeth remain primitive

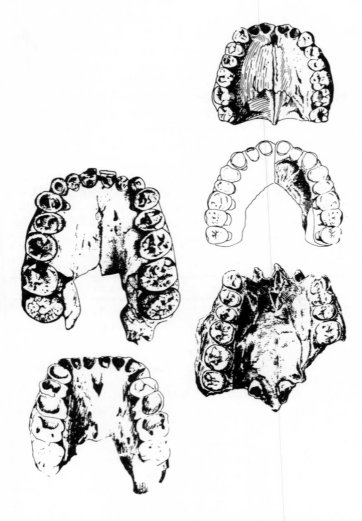

FIG. 59. Upper jaws of australopithecines (left) and hominines (right). Lower left: *"Paranthropus"* (Swartkrans); upper left: *Zinjanthropus* (Olduvai); lower right: *Pithecanthropus modjokertensis* (Java); right center: Peking man; upper right: modern *Homo sapiens.* Other forms at bottom. All the jaws have been reduced to the same scale.

The different trends in the evolution of man are best reflected in the development of the upper jaws, shown quite clearly in figure 59. In the huge jaw of *Zinjanthropus,* the tiny canines are in marked contrast to the rest; *P. modjokertensis* with its "monkey gap" and diverging rows of teeth is much more sharply divided from Peking man (and *Homo erectus*) than the latter is from *Homo sapiens.*

Neanderthal Man and the Origins of Homo Sapiens

Neanderthal men represent the morphological and evolutionary link between *Pithecanthropus* and modern man. We say "Neanderthal men" rather than "Neanderthal man" because they represent different types that can be divided into a number of branches.

The European finds can be fitted into three groups according to the associated fauna:

1. An older warm-climate fauna, including the forest elephant (*Elephas antiquus*), the Etruscan rhinoceros (*Rhinoceros etruscus*), and the elk (*Alces latifrons*), etc. Certainly older than the Mindel-Riss interglacial. To this belongs the single Heidelberg lower jaw which we mentioned during our discussion of *Pithecanthropus.*

2. A younger warm-climate fauna, including *Elephas antiquus* and *Rhinoceros mercki.* Interglacial fauna and Riss interstadial fauna.

3. A more recent cold-climate fauna including the mammoth (*Elephas primigenius*), the wooly rhinoceros (*Coelodanta tichorhinus*), the reindeer (*Rangifer tarandus*), and the cave bear (*Ursus spelaeus*), etc. Fauna of Würm glaciation, when men lived in caves. No European men are known from the Riss and Mindel glacials themselves.

Neanderthal man was first so called after an incomplete skeleton discovered by J. C. Fuhlrott, a teacher from Elbersfeld, in the Neander valley, not far from Düsseldorf. The skeleton was dug out of the clay of a small cave opened up by quarry workers. No animal bones or tools were found in its vicinity. The skull was fairly squat and had pronounced brow ridges. Although Fuhlrott and Schaaffhausen, a Bonn anatomist, were convinced that the find was very ancient and represented man's primitive precursor, they were overruled by R. Virchow. Hence it was left to an Englishman to classify the find and to name it *Homo neanderthalensis* King, 1864. The scientific world at large accepted Neanderthal as an Ice Age man only after similar remains were discovered in Belgium.

The real, classical or extreme Neanderthal man is, as we know today, the exclusive product of the Würm glaciation (Würm I). His remains, some in a state of excellent preservation, have been dug up in a number of European sites. The most important finds were:

> Germany: Neanderthal, 1856; the classic find; skull top and skeleton remains.
>
> Belgium: Spy, 1886; two skulls and skeleton remains.
>
> France: La Chapelle aux Saints, 1908; complete adult skeleton; Le Moustier, 1908; complete adolescent skeleton. La Quina, 1908–21; mainly skulls, including a child's; La Ferrassie (Fig. 60), 1909–21, skulls; Arcy sur Cur, 1949–51, excellent jaw fragments; Regourdon, 1957, excellent lower jaw.
>
> Britain: Jersey, 1910–11, interesting set of teeth.
>
> Italy: Monte Circeo, 1939; sacrificial skull.
>
> Greece: Petralona near Salonica (1960); finest and most primitive Neanderthal skull found in Europe; no lower jaw. Huge upper jaw with advanced dentition. Occiput not rounded as in other European types but coming to a point as with African and Javanese Neanderthalers. Age:

Würm (?). Only a preliminary account has been published.

Soviet Union: Kiyik Koba (Crimea), 1924; isolated skeleton fragments including a complete foot; Teshik Tash (Uzbek, U.S.S.R.), 1938, child grave.

All these finds come from caves. The associated culture is called "Mousterian" after the French cave of that name.

The classical Neanderthal man is characterized by pronounced brow ridges, a squat skull top, and a cranial capacity (1,350–1,723 cc. according to Gieseler) which is comparable to that of modern man (1,350–1,500 cc.). The back of the skull is rounded, the face is ogre-like, the nasal bones are well developed, and the nasal aperture is large. The molars are big, strongly wrinkled, and have deep pulp cavities (taurodontism); the premolars and canines are no larger than those of modern man. The chin is absent. The arm and femur are slightly arched; the leg is generally short. Estimated size of body: 5 feet to 5 feet 4 inches (Fig. 61).

Classical Neanderthal man was supplanted by *H. sapiens.* (Fig. 62). The two have no direct genetic connection. The classical is a terminal type adapted to an extremely

Measurements of the classic Neanderthal skull

	Maximum length (mm.)	Maximum width (mm.)	Index	Distance from basion to bregma	Cranial capacity (in cc.)
Neanderthal	199	147	73.9	—	1,500(e)
Spy I	200	140	71.3	—	1,562
La Quina	203	138	68.2	122(e)	1,350
La Chapelle aux Saints	208	156	75	131	1,620

After Weidenreich (1943) and Gieseler (1957)   [(e) = *estimate*]

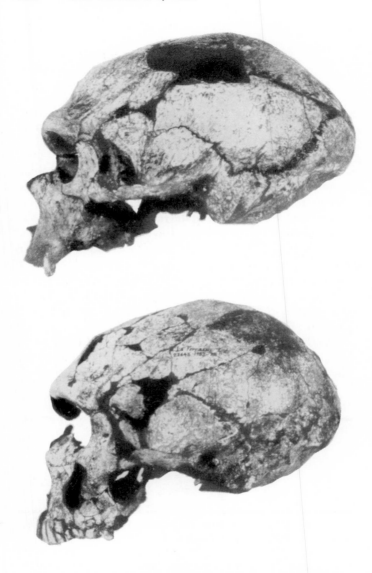

FIG. 60. Two classical Neanderthal skulls. Top: La Chapelle aux Saints; Below: La Ferrassie. (After L. Pales.)

FIG. 61. Reconstruction of Neanderthal men. (After a drawing by W. Wandel.)

cold climate, and our own precursors must be sought among the earlier types. Before we do that, however, we must discuss yet another type, which might be called "tropical" by comparison. Our knowledge of it is based on the following three finds:

> Africa: Broken Hill, Rhodesia, 1921. Well-preserved skull lacking lower jaw; some skeleton fragments. Saldanha Bay (near Cape Town), 1953; a

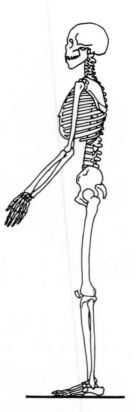

FIG. 62. Skeleton of modern man.

skull top and more recently a small lower jaw fragment.

Asia: Ngandong, Central Java, 1931–33. Eleven damaged skull tops without facial bones or jaws; two tibias.

The Broken Hill remains were discovered in a cave; the rest in the open.

The best preserved find is the Broken Hill skull (Fig. 63), from which we know that its owner had the largest face of any fossil man. By its side lay a few scattered fragments of bones, stone implements, and animal remains of modern appearance. The Ngandong find was made on the 75 foot terrace of the Solo River (whence it is also known as Solo man); its accompanying fauna still consisted of

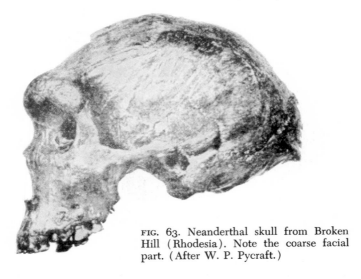

FIG. 63. Neanderthal skull from Broken Hill (Rhodesia). Note the coarse facial part. (After W. P. Pycraft.)

extinct elephants (*Stegodon*) and hippopotami, but was clearly more modern than that of Trinil. The find consists of eleven skulls, many severely damaged, two tibias, and nothing else. The primitive stone implements consisting of crude flakes and rounded shots are reminiscent of the Broken Hill industry. In addition, there were some bone tools. The Saldanha find (Fig. 64), finally, consisted of an incomplete skull similar in size to, but more solid than, the Broken Hill skull. Judging from the associated implements and the many extinct animals it is the older of the two, so that Saldanha man may well have been the direct ancestor of Rhodesian man.

All these skulls have a thick though not very prominent brow ridge, flattened brain cases, and powerful nuchal crests on the occipital bone for the attachment of the exceptionally strong neck muscles.

From his cranial capacity (just over 1,000 cc. in Ngandong I, VI, X, and XI), we know that Solo man (Fig. 65) must have been the most primitive of the whole group.

FIG. 64. Skull roof of Saldanha man. (After R. Singer.)

Measurements of the tropical Neanderthal skull

	Maximum length	Maximum width	Index	Distance from basion to bregma	Brain capacity (in cc.)
Rhodesia	210	144.5	69.4	129	1,325
Saldhanha	200	144	69	—	1,200(e)
Ngandong VI	193	140	73.3	123(e)	1,035
Ngandong XI	202	141	70.8	123	1,060
Ngandong V	219.5	144	66.2	131(e)	1,255

After Weidenreich and Singer   [(e) = estimate]

Although all the Solo foreheads are higher than that of *Pithecanthropus*, the skull of some types—and particularly that of Ngandong XI (Fig. 66)—is broadest near the temporal fossae. This contrasts with the skulls of other Neanderthal and modern men which have their maximum widths higher up in the parietal region. Solo man has an

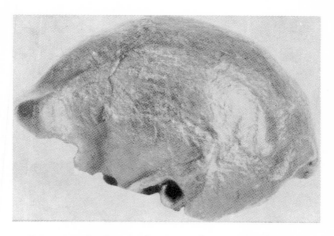

FIG. 65. Braincase of Solo man from Ngandong (Central Java).

uncommonly large mastoid process. (Oddly enough the process is barely present in Pithecanthropus II which, in this respect, is closer to the anthropoid apes than to man, even though its glenoid fossa which receives the condyle of the lower jaw is deepened and constructed like man's.) Solo man's foramen magnum is oval and inclined to the horizontal.

Weidenreich's claim that Solo man is a direct descendant of *Pithecanthropus* is highly controversial. First of all, the geological distance between the two is very difficult to evaluate, and then Java has been the melting pot of so many different races since the Mesolithic (Wadjaks, Sampungs, Proto-Malayans, Malayans, pygmies, Veddahs) that no linear development of mankind can be expected in this marginal region of Asia.

However, we must now return to the North African and European finds. They can be divided into two groups, though not always quite easily. One group leads to the earliest Neanderthal man (Fig. 67) and may be called the pre-Neanderthal series; the other leads indirectly to

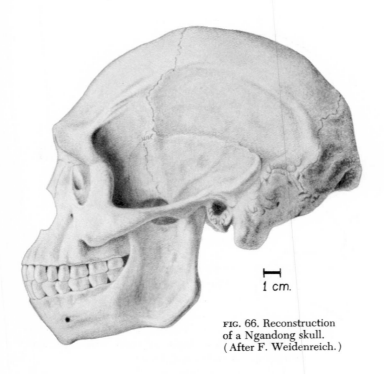

1 cm.

FIG. 66. Reconstruction
of a Ngandong skull.
(After F. Weidenreich.)

Homo sapiens and will be referred to as the presapiens series.

The following remains of pre-Neanderthal man date from the last interglacial:

> Germany: Ehringsdorf near Weimar. First skull (since lost) discovered as early as 1871; skull fragments and fragment of femur 1908; lower jaw 1914; lower jaw and fragments of child skeleton 1916; female braincase 1925. Taubach near Weimar: two teeth (1887 and 1892).
>
> Yugoslavia: Krapina 1895–1905. More than 500 smashed fragments of at least 13 (possibly 40) individuals.

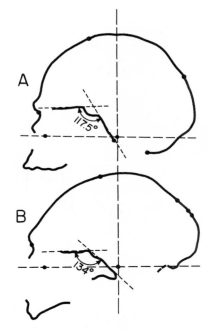

FIG. 67. The shape of
the skull of (A) Palestine
Neanderthal man (Skhul V)
and (B) extreme
Neanderthal man from
Mt. Circeo.
(After F. Clark Howell.)

Czechoslovakia: Ganovce 1926. Brain cast and fragments of radius and fibula.

Italy: Saccopastore near Rome: female skull 1929; upper jaw and fragments of male skull, 1935.

The Ehringsdorf, Taubach, and Ganovce finds come from open sites; the Krapina find from a cave or rock-shelter; the Saccopastore find from a gravel deposit.

The Saccopastore skull (Fig. 68) is the best-preserved of all. It is short, narrow and relatively squat, and has an estimated cranial capacity of 1,200 cc. The brow ridge is not very prominent, the orbits and nose are wide. The Ehringsdorf skull is very fragmentary, and the reconstructions by Weidenreich (1928) and Kleinschmidt (1958) are incompatible. The skull is oval and high, and Weidenreich has estimated its capacity at 1,450 cc.

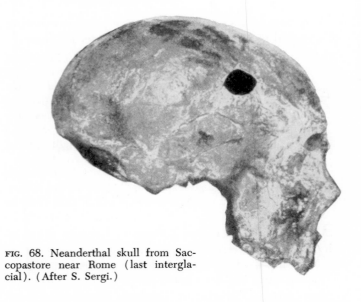

FIG. 68. Neanderthal skull from Saccopastore near Rome (last interglacial). (After S. Sergi.)

Kötschke has argued that the two Ehringsdorf jaws are
so different that they must have belonged to two different
types. The Krapina jaws and teeth are well-known from
the classical account by Gorjanovic-Kramberger. The
teeth (like those of Taubach—Fig. 69) are exceptionally
wrinkled, and X-ray pictures reveal an extremely deep
pulp cavity.

The above finds must probably be coupled with the following discoveries of rather uncertain geological age:

> Gibraltar: Forbes Quarry 1844: female (?)
> skull. Devil's Tower 1926: fragments of child's
> skull.
> Spain: Banolas near Gerona 1887: lower jaw.
> The Gibraltar finds were made in caves or rock
> shelters, the Banolas jaw comes from a tuff.

Though the Gibraltar predated the Neanderthal find, it
was not identified until much later. Its skull resembles the
one from Saccopastore fairly well.

A number of lower jaws indicate the possible existence of a special group of North African Neanderthal men:

> Sidi-Abderrahman, Morocco, 1955. Fragments of a massive lower jaw with large molars (length of the three molars 39.2 mm.). From about the beginning of the third African pluvial corresponding roughly with the beginning of the Riss glaciation.
>
> Temara near Rabat, Morocco, 1958. Massive lower jaw with rudimentary chin. Length of three molars 38 mm.
>
> Haua Fteah, Cyrenaica, 1952–54. Back sections of two lower jaws and two Neanderthaloid molars.
>
> All finds come from cave debris or cliffs near the coast.

Vallois has stressed that differences between the symphyses of the three jaws suggest that North African Neanderthal man must have developed along distinct lines.

All the finds we have listed so far seem to belong to either "extreme" or else to "tropical" Neanderthal man, and to their direct precursors. This brings us to the problem of our own ancestors.

A very important, but fragmentary, find comes from Hungary: Vertészöllös near Budapest, 1960. Two teeth; one strikingly large occipital bone.

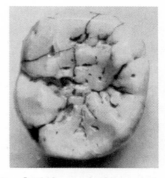

FIG. 69. Lower molar of Taubach Neanderthal man, highly magnified. (W. Molison.)

The site is a travertine hill surrounded by flat country. Unfortunately, the larger part of the complex had been levelled by the time its importance was recognized in 1963. The fauna included *Trogontherium* and *Epimachairodus* as well as a host of rodents. Kretzoi has dated it back to the Mindel of Bihar, which would make it only a little more recent than Mauer and Mosbach. The find included many crushed and singed bones but no charcoal remains. The culture is most appropriately described as "micro-pebble" since only a few of the implements were larger than 5 cm. Most of them are flakes and choppers, simply chipped on one or two edges, and would never have been regarded as artifacts had they been dug up in isolation. They were primitive enough to have come from Africa rather than from Europe.

The human remains recovered by Vertes and recently described by Thoma (1946) include an isolated lower deciduous canine with a pronounced (and hence archaic) mesiodistal diameter, and an isolated occiput of modern appearance, except that it comes to a point and has an (archaic) torus occipitalis. It is vaguely reminiscent of the skull of Neanderthal man from Petralona, Greece, but is probably older.

> Steinheim on the Murr, Würtemberg, 1933. Complete female (?) skull except for lower jaw. Surrounded by warm-climate fauna. Probable date Mindel-Riss interglacial. River gravel.

Except for the Heidelberg lower jaw, Berkheimer's Steinheim skull is the most important German find. The left side of the skull is smashed, probably by force, and the foramen magnum seems to have been opened up. Since no other parts of the skeleton were found in the vicinity, the skull was probably a head-hunter's trophy.

The brow ridge is comparable to that of *Sinanthropus*, but the skull is not only much higher than that of *Sinanthropus* but has its maximum width (132 mm.) in the

FIG. 70. Lateral views of Steinheim skull (cast; top) and of Australian aborigine skull (bottom).

parietal region. As a result it looks much narrower than that of "extreme" Neanderthal man (maximum width: 138–158 mm.). Moreover, as Gieseler has shown, the Neanderthal skull looks broader and rounder from the back than the (rather pentagonal) Steinheim skull (Fig. 70).

The length of the Steinheim skull is 185 mm., and its cranial capacity must have been between 1,100 and 1,200 cc. The molars are small and not very wrinkled; the front set of teeth is unfortunately missing. The orbits are set wide apart; the root of the nose is set well back like that of modern man. The skull has a cheek groove, unlike that of Neanderthal man.

It has often been stressed that the Steinheim skull forms the great divide in man's evolution; by underplaying its Neanderthal characteristics, we can easily change it into *Homo sapiens;* by exaggerating these characteristics we can turn it into "extreme" Neanderthal man. However, the *sapiens* characteristics (root of nose, cheek groove) seem to be the more pronounced of the two.

> Swanscombe (near London). Occipital bone 1935; left parietal bone 1936; right parietal bone 1955. All from the same skull. Mindel-Riss interglacial.
>
> From the 100 foot terrace of the Lower Thames.

The skull was found in the Middle Gravels of the "Barnsfield pit" together with many remains of a warm-climate mammalian fauna, and with flint implements of Middle Acheulian type. Unfortunately, no tools can as yet be associated with the Steinheim skull.

FIG. 71. Top view of Montmaurin lower jaw.

The back of the Swanscombe skull is as rounded as that of the Steinheim. All fragments of the two are comparable, though the Swanscombe bones are a little thicker. Unfortunately, the frontal bone—the most important standard of comparison—is missing.

Neither in Steinheim nor in Swanscombe has any part of the lower jaw been dug up, though the following find may possibly fill the gap.

> Montmaurin (Haute-Garonne), France, 1949. Complete lower jaw with all six molars. Highly fossilized. Associated with warm-climate fauna. Probably Mindel-Riss interglacial.

According to Vallois, the Montmaurin jaw (Fig. 71) is the oldest discovered in France and, apart from the Mauer (Heidelberg) jaw, the oldest of all. Although it is not as massive as the Mauer, the two are alike in the height and angle of their symphyses (Heidelberg jaw: 70°; Montmaurin jaw: 73°; Neanderthal jaw: 80°). The Montmaurin symphysis itself is shorter than that of both Heidelberg and Neanderthal man, but represents a morphological half-way stage between them (Fig. 72). The teeth are moderately wrinkled, and the last molar is the largest of the row—a particularly primitive trait. Montmaurin and Steinheim teeth are similar in size and mark-

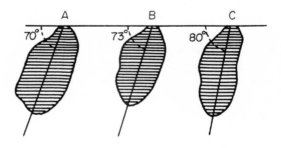

FIG. 72. Symphysial cross-sections of (A) Heidelberg, (B) Montmaurin, (C) Neanderthal lower jaws. Half natural size. (After H. V. Vallois.)

ings, but the Montmaurin lower jaw looks the broader of the two. The difference may, however, be purely sexual, for while the Steinheim skull is assumed to be female, the Montmaurin lower jaw may well have been male.

Unfortunately, the geological ages of the Montmaurin and Steinheim skulls are not known with any certainty. Vallois has classified Montmaurin with the pre-Neanderthal series.

Two finds from Southwestern France continue to puzzle the experts:

> Fontéchevade (Charante) 1947. Small fragment of frontal bone with superior orbital ridge (I); a larger fragment with upper edge of forehead and most of the parietal bones (II).

The two finds were dug up by Mlle. G. Henri-Martin from a cave layer covered by a massive layer of calcareous sinter. The site also contained the remains of a warm-climate fauna corresponding to the last interglacial. The human fragments lay under the layer of sinter but in front of the cave. Their fluorine content is identical with that of the associated animal remains; hence they must have been deposited at about the same time.

The largest crushed fragment suggests a receding forehead; the smaller fragments (belonging to two individuals) indicate that the skulls differed from the Neanderthal in having no brow ridges. Hence Vallois has coupled Fontéchevade with Swanscombe man as true representatives of the pre-*sapiens* series.

Since the frontal region of Swanscombe man is missing, Vallois' view has been challenged by Clark Howell, who concluded from a personal investigation of the fragments that they are more likely to represent a true Neanderthal type. The issue can only be decided by the discovery of fresh material.

In addition, we have a far more important series of Palestinian skeletons, providing indirect proof of the existence of early *sapiens* in the Middle East. These finds date from the beginning of the Würm glaciation and not, as is often said, from the end of that period. They are collectively known as the Carmel skeletons.

> Palestine: Mugharet el-Zuttiyeh near Genezareth, 1925: Skull fragments (Galilean skull).
>
> Kafzeh near Nazareth, 1933–35: Remains of six individuals (not yet described).
>
> Mugharet es-Skhul, 1931–32: Remains of ten individuals.
>
> Mugharet et-Tabun, 1931–32: Skeleton of a woman aged about 30 years; male lower jaw; skeleton remains and teeth; from different levels.
>
> All discovered in caves or rock-shelters.

The Carmel finds are the most important and most hotly contested of all the Palestinian discoveries. They come from two caves and from the debris in front of them. The Tabun woman was small (just under 5 feet); her skull was relatively short (183 mm.) and low (115 mm.). The brain capacity was roughly 1,270 cc. The marked brow ridges and well-rounded occipital arch resemble those of the female skulls of Krapina, Saccopastore, and Gibraltar.

The remains of (at least) 10 individuals found in the nearby Skhul caves consist mainly of scattered parts, damaged before they were deposited. Two men, Skhul IV and V, were tall (5 feet 11 inches to 6 feet and possibly more). The skulls are long (192–206 mm.); the cranial capacity is more than 1,500 cc. All still have brow ridges, but the lower jaws have projecting chins—a strange mixture of Neanderthal and *sapiens* characteristics. If we assume Tabun and Skhul to have been contemporaries, as is sometimes done, the differences between them are far greater than those between the individuals of any known race.

Two possible reasons may explain this strange phenomenon: either the Neanderthal type had become unstable and was on the point of turning into *sapiens,* or else Carmel man was a mixture of the two. Both possibilities

have been considered by various experts. We have
adopted the second view after a careful examination of
the associated implements. It seems reasonable to infer
the emergence of new human types from the appearance
of new stone cultures since, in European caves, extreme
Neanderthal man is always associated with Mousterian
implements (flake tool and hand industries), and *Homo
sapiens* (Cro-Magnon man) with Aurignacian implements.

Now, Rust's excavations in the Near East have shown
the existence of an early pre-Aurignacian culture diluted
with quasi-Mousterian influences. This culture was particularly widespread in the Carmel complex and is often
difficult to isolate because of the complex structure of
the layers. According to Rust (1958) the Mousterio-pre-
Aurignacian is a bastard culture, with mixed Neanderthal
and *sapiens*-like elements, and explains why some of the
Carmel skeletons were of the bastard type.

As we saw, man, from now on *Homo sapiens,* appeared
in Europe immediately after but not out of classical Neanderthal man. The Carmel finds indicate that he must have
reached Europe from the East. When that happened will
only be known when and if further material is brought to
light.

We can now attempt to reconstruct man's family tree.
In the past, everything seemed exceedingly simple; Heidelberg, Neanderthal, and *Homo sapiens* represented so
many points connected by a straight line. Since then, new
finds have complicated the original scheme considerably.
Even the *Pithecanthropus* group had to be split into a
number of "types," and Neanderthal man into still more.
To what extent these types represented (eugenically com-
patible) "races" or incompatible species can rarely be
judged. We must not forget that while all the races of
modern mankind are coeval, and clearly not too differentiated to crossbreed, fossil types are often separated by in-
determinate intervals of time. Only when fossils have

been dated absolutely by the recent isotope method may we gain a better idea of their duration.

In any case, the agents of evolution are not so much single individuals as isolated or interrelated groups. Hence our family tree has the many twists and turns constituting Breitinger's diagram (Fig. 73).

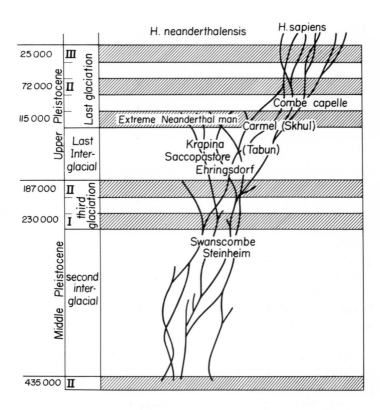

FIG. 73. Probable relationship between *Homo neandertha-lensis* and *Homo sapiens,* inferred from fossil finds. (After E. Breitinger.)

IV. TOWARD MAN

Having reviewed the various human fossil discoveries, we can now attempt to summarize what we know of man's evolution.

We are struck first of all by the widespread Old World distribution of the various groups that played a part in man's origins. The pongids, today limited to Sumatra, Borneo, and Central and West Africa, once roamed from Europe in the west to China in the east and to Central Africa in the south. The australopithecines are apparently a purely South African group but may have originated in Asia. Teeth found in China may have belonged to them; further, they have striking morphological similarities with the Javanese *Meganthropus*. Fossils from Java, China, North Africa, and possibly from Europe, show that the *Pithecanthropus* group, too, must have had a far wider distribution than was formerly thought. If we take it that, like the Pongidae, the oldest men lived mainly on fruit, they must have been limited to the "tropics," which in the Miocene embraced Southern and Central Europe.

The Javanese *Pithecanthropus* has his temperate-climate counterpart in *Sinanthropus*, who migrated north at about the time when "classical" Neanderthal man had become fully adapted to life under Arctic conditions.

The chronological order and morphological development of these types is the key to human evolution. That evolution seems much more straightforward now that we have dismissed Piltdown man as a forgery. At this point, we must say a few words on the Piltdown subject.

Between 1912 and 1915, a number of important human fossil remains were dug up in Piltdown, Sussex (England). They included a high-domed skull without brow ridges and with the prominent forehead of modern man. The same site produced an apelike upper canine and an apelike lower jaw with a damaged canine section, all of which were alleged to belong to the original skull. The discoverer of the skull and the other fragments was Charles Dawson, an amateur archaeologist. He took the pieces to the British Museum, where they were most carefully studied by the eminent paleontologist Arthur Smith Woodward. The associated fauna was found to be of an extremely ancient type. In 1913, Smith Woodward described the skull as *Eoanthropus dawsoni*. Though the simian lower jaw remained a puzzle, *Eoanthropus* was considered the oldest of all men (possibly Tertiary), and therefore proof that modern man is more ancient than was formerly believed.

Since none of the subsequent Chinese and Javanese discoveries bore any resemblance to Piltdown man, it seemed that mankind must have evolved along two independent lines. While *Homo sapiens* was said to be the direct descendent of *Eoanthropus* and of the slightly more recent Galley Hill man, *Pithecanthropus,* Heidelberg and Neanderthal man were taken for the end products of a second, blind, line of evolution.

This theory was disturbed by Oakley in 1954 when he measured the age of Piltdown man by the fluorine method. This method is based on the fact that bones absorb fluorine from the water of the subsoil at a steady rate. The proportion of fluorine in them therefore indicates their age. Oakley showed that many of the animal fragments surrounding the Piltdown skull had a very high fluorine content but the human remains had practically none. Weiner, a young Oxford anthropologist, then examined all the Piltdown finds with a detective's eye and concluded that the whole business must have been a deliberate fraud. The skull and the jaw had been artificially "aged" with potassium bichromate; the lower jaw was that of an ape (probably an orangutan as Weidenreich had previously suspected it to be on purely morphological grounds). The forgers had removed the canine and had filed down the molars to make them look human. The upper canine, too, had been filed down, and, as Oakley discovered later, the alleged Piltdown fragments had been collected from all over the place and probably included the tusk of a North African elephant. Even the tools "discovered" in Piltdown were not of local origin. In short, the forgers had set to work with a will.

Oakley's method also enabled paleontologists to classify the Galley Hill and other doubtful finds as recent, and hence rendered greater service to paleontology than many a new discovery. We have dwelled on the Piltdown affair at such length because it was considered crucial in all texts published after the "discovery" and before 1954.

We can now return to the *Pithecanthropus* group. Their wide distribution, first recognized a few years ago, makes it difficult to say when and where Neanderthal man emerged from them and whether they represent the roots of modern humanity. Weidenreich has argued that *Sinanthropus* (Fig. 74) is related to the Mongolian race and *Pithecanthropus* to the Australian aborigines. His main criterion was the spatular formation of the incisor which Peking man shares with modern Mongolians. Since then, however, it has appeared that *Pithecanthropus modjokertensis* also has spatular incisors. In fact, the striking resemblance between modern races and their ability to crossbreed successfully suggest very strongly that the geographical divi-

sions of modern mankind occurred after the crystalliza-
tion of the "*Homo sapiens*" type.

Man's superiority over the rest of the animal kingdom
rests on a number of characteristics. The chief are his absolutely and relatively large brain and his very sensitive,
movable, and versatile hand which, as Kälin has put it,
has become man's cultural organ.

Little is known about its evolution. Apes use their hands
purely for grasping, and we cannot tell whether their relatively short and inflexible thumb is a primitive or a specialized characteristic.

We know that a marked increase in cranial capacity
occurred in the Pleistocene. Though we have explained
that the australopithecines cannot be considered as precursors of man, there is no doubt that their cranial capacity was greater than that of modern pongids. We say
"modern" intentionally since we assume that *Gigantopithecus* probably had a cranial capacity corresponding to
that of early man. The cranial capacity of the australo-

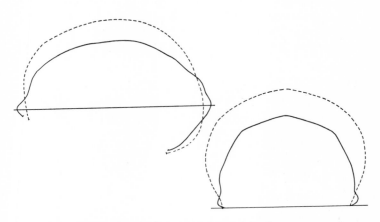

FIG. 74. Increase of cranial capacity from *Sinanthropus* to modern
man (stippled). Top: longitudinal section; bottom: cross section.
Greatly reduced in size. (After F. Weidenreich.)

pithecines was unduly exaggerated when it was first published. The most recent estimates are shown in the table
on page 72.

In connection with brain capacity, we must briefly
discuss the question of body size. In the living higher primates, the size of the teeth is an indication of their stat-
ure. The chimpanzee has the smallest, the gorilla the largest set of teeth; the orangutan's is intermediate. The same
relations must be assumed to have held in fossil hominids
and pongids, viz. *Meganthropus* and *Gigantopithecus,* for
which Chinese paleontologists claim a size of 10 feet. On
the other hand, it has been argued that large teeth are
not necessarily proof of a large body. It strikes me that
we had best suspend judgment on the whole matter until
the missing limb bones themselves are discovered. In any
case, *Gigantopithecus,* whose teeth are larger than those
of the gorilla, is likely to have had a larger cranial capacity as well. The development of cranial capacity may be
gathered from the following table:

Cranial capacity of fossil hominids

Pithecanthropus II	775 cc.
Sinanthropus III	915 cc.
Pithecanthropus I	935 cc.
Sinanthropus XI	1,015 cc.
Solo VI	1,035 cc.
Solo XI	1,060 cc.
Solo IX	1,135 cc.
Sinanthropus X	1,225 cc.
Solo V	1,255 cc.
Tabun I	1,270 cc.
Gibraltar	1,300 cc.
La Quina	1,350 cc.
Neanderthal	1,370 cc.

After Weidenreich (1944)

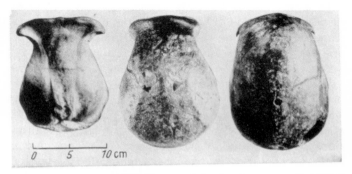

FIG. 75. Increasing prominence of forehead associated with decreasing constriction behind the orbits. Left: Gorilla; center: *Pithecanthropus erectus* II; right: modern man.

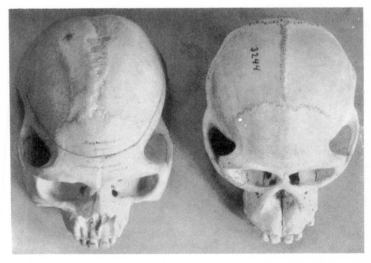

FIG. 76. The marked constriction behind the orbits of anthropoid apes (Orangutan; right) is also found in microcephalic skulls of modern man (Javanese; left).

FIG. 77. The steepening of the forehead. Left: *Sinanthropus;* center: Neanderthal man; right: modern man. (After F. Weidenreich.)

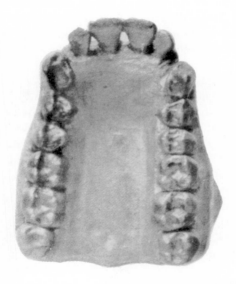

FIG. 78. The development of the upper dental arch 1: *Sivapithecus sivalensis* from the Pliocene of India. Jaw of a primitive pongid. Upper canines less specialized than those of modern anthropoid apes. Rows of teeth roughly parallel. Natural size. (Reconstruction by M. Hellman.)

Later (La Chapelle) Neanderthal man's cranial capacity of 1,610, cc. was higher than that of recent Europeans —as Boule put it, La Chapelle man was more brainy than the average Parisian.

A growing brain went hand in hand with the gradual steepening of the forehead (Figs. 75–77) and the gradual disappearance of the continuous brow ridge, present in all types up to Neanderthal man.

The steady increase in man's brain capacity during the Pleistocene is a measure of his general evolution. Another factor to be considered is the ratio of brain to body weight. It is impossible to make comparisons between modern and fossil man, but studies have been made of anthropoid apes and modern man. While the newly born have a comparable brain to body weight ratio, the relative weight of the brain in adult man is more than twice that in the anthropoid ape.

Ratio of brain to body weight

	Newly born	Adult
Orangutan (female)	8.61	0.93
(male)		0.56
Gorilla (male)		0.57
Chimpanzee (female)		0.87
(male)	8.21	0.86
Man (female)		2.11±
(male)	9.90	2.07±

After Schultz (1957) (±Negro)

The newly-born ape resembles man not only in absolute brain weight, but also in having its foramen magnum directly beneath the skull. In man, the foramen remains in this position throughout life and helps to balance the head on the vertebral column. In apes, which walk on all fours, the foramen gradually shifts to the back of the skull. In order to balance the head and the massive face and snout, apes have developed huge muscles near the base of the skull. The heavy lower jaw of apes with its great canines (Fig. 78) also calls for strong muscles, so that the ape skull gradually gets packed with muscle tissue. All of this causes strengthening of the skull with bony crests in the occipital and sometimes in the sagittal regions. These crests are most pronounced in the gorilla. All human skulls have a temporal groove on either side of the skull. The two grooves never meet, though they are fairly close in *Pithecanthropus*. In *Australopithecus,* on the other hand, the grooves join to form a crest in the anterior part of the parietal bone.

The forehead of young anthropoid apes sweeps up much like that of human adults, but as the ape grows older its muscles tend to flatten the skull. The young child, on the other hand, has its overlapping forehead pulled upward and straight.

The skull of the average man is roughly 1.5 mm. thick, and that of apes is not much thicker. Hence it is odd that both *Pithecanthropus* and Neanderthal (particularly Solo) man should have had such thick skulls (more than 1 cm.). From photographs it appears that the australopithecines, too, had very thick skulls. The significance of this exclusive trait of early mankind escapes us, though *Pithecanthropus* and Neanderthal man may well have developed thicker skulls to withstand the pressure of their increasing brains. In fact, their brain casts show more detail than those of modern man.

Differences in length and breadth of fossilized human skulls are comparable with modern variations. However, the skulls of *Sinanthropus* and *Pithecanthropus* were exceptionally low.

Increases in brain size since the beginning of the Pleistocene led to a progressive thinning of the skull bones and to a resulting increase in cranial capacity. At the same time, the skull began to grow upwards, the forehead part became steeper, and the brow ridges began to disappear.

The continuous torus supraorbitalis gave way to two slight ridges above the orbits, the tori superciliaris. The face came to lie more directly beneath the skull cap.

Moreover, the face became smaller, the orbits grew rounder and closer together, and the nasal aperture became narrower and dropped lower. The reduction of the face was accompanied by a reduction of the jaws, or conversely. As we saw, *Pithecanthropus modjokertensis, Sinanthropus,* and *Atlanthropus* had much larger teeth than modern man. The largest set of all was that of the *Meganthropus.* The dentition of *Pithecanthropus modjokertensis* is distinguished by a primitive jaw with all the teeth in a plane and both rows converging to the front (Fig. 79).

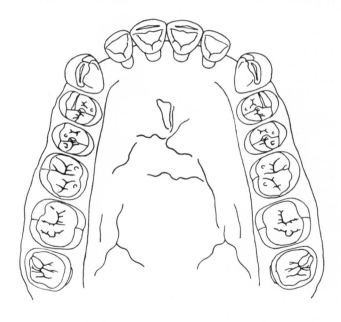

FIG. 79. The development of the upper dental arch 2: *Pithecanthropus modjokertensis* from the Lower Pleistocene of Central Java. Primitive hominid arch. Canine prominent; "monkey gap" still present; rows converge towards the front. Natural size.

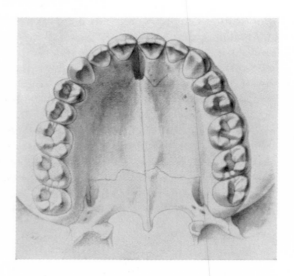

FIG. 80. The development of the upper dental arch 3: *Homo sapiens*. Arch typically rounded; weak canine, no gaps. Natural size. (Ideal set, after E. Selenka.)

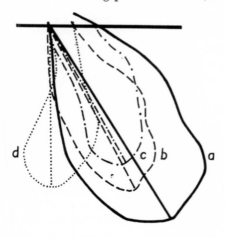

FIG. 81. Size and inclination of symphysis in hominids. (a) *Meganthropus;* (b) Heidelberg; (c) *Sinanthropus;* (d) modern man (Chinese). 1⅕ natural size. (After F. Weidenreich.)

It also has a pointed canine, a gap between the canines and incisors—the notorious "monkey gap"—and a dominant second molar. Hence *Pithecanthropus* had the most primitive human upper jaw known. From *Sinanthropus* on, the dental arch is closed and more or less parabolical like our own (Fig. 80).

Homo sapiens is the only man with a "positive" chin. In the course of evolution, the human jaw line underwent a progressive bending back, i.e., its symphysial angle increased (Fig. 81).

Angle of Inclination of Symphysis

Orangutan (W)	44°
Gorilla (W)	47°
Chimpanzee (W)	50°
Ramapithecus (W)	57°
Meganthropus (W)	58°
Sinanthropus H (W)	63°
Heidelberg (W)	63°
Krapina H (W)	63°
Rabat (V)	65°
Atlanthropus III (A)	70°
Montmaurin (V)	73°
Austr. abor. (W)	75°
Modern man (W)	91°

After Weidenreich (1945) W;
Arambourg (1956) A; and Vallois (1958) V

The evolution of the rest of the skeleton can be reviewed very briefly—very little is known about it. The famous femur of *Pithecanthropus erectus,* which, by the way, showed traces of arthritis, is indistinguishable in form from that of modern man. From its length, we can deduce that its owner must have been 5 feet 7 inches tall. We have already seen that the skeleton of classical Neanderthal man is distinguished from that of modern man by its curved femur and humerus and by other peculiarities, and that classical Neanderthal man must represent a special

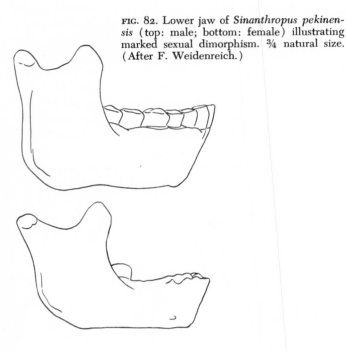

FIG. 82. Lower jaw of *Sinanthropus pekinensis* (top: male; bottom: female) illustrating marked sexual dimorphism. ¾ natural size. (After F. Weidenreich.)

side line. Here we must discuss yet another special phenomenon: sexual dimorphism. While female orangutans and gorillas are only half the weight of the males, female chimpanzees and gibbons weigh roughly 10 per cent less than the males, and modern women about 17 per cent less than modern men. Comparative figures are not, of course, available for fossil men, but we have seen that male and female *Sinanthropus* jaws differ so greatly in size that they were originally mistaken for the jaws of different species (Fig. 82). Most probably sexual dimorphism was much greater in early than in modern man.

We have also seen that the proportions of simian limbs, adapted to arboreal life, differ considerably from man's. The simian femur and humerus are roughly of equal length, while man's femur is some 25 per cent longer than his humerus. According to Weidenreich, the difference was only 20 per cent in *Sinanthropus* (see Fig. 83). In this respect, as well as in the proportions of his skull and teeth, Peking man was therefore strikingly "apelike."

Using modern man with his spacious and rounded cranium, steep forehead, closed dental arch, relatively small

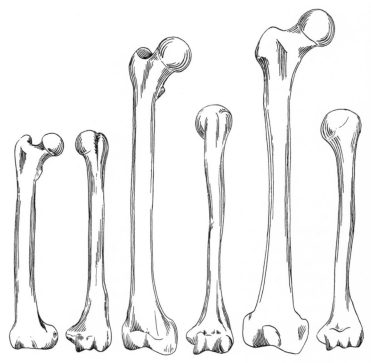

FIG. 83. Relative sizes of femur and humerus in the chimpanzee (left); *Sinanthropus* (center); and modern man (right). (After F. Weidenreich.)

teeth, and chin as a standard, we find that our fossil predecessors were far less "human." They had a smaller brain case, a brow ridge, a receding forehead, and a different dental arch which sometimes showed a gap. Their teeth were large and strongly wrinkled; they had no chin. Instead of "less human" we might have said "more primitive" or "simian." However, "primitive" had best be reserved for those characteristics which man shares with the apes, and "simian" for exclusive ape characteristics. By modern human standards, many characteristics of fossil apes are quite "unsimian": *Proconsul* lacked a brow ridge, *Ramapithecus* and *Gigantopithecus* had smaller canines than the existing anthropoid apes. In many cases, it is not so much a given characteristic itself as its evolutionary significance which concerns us most, and it is here that the main differences between pongids and hominids seem to lie. Thus modern man has lost certain primitive characteristics, e.g., the enlarged canines of fossil man which are "simian" in their extreme form.

Man has so much in common with the large anthropoid apes that they must have shared a common ancestor in the distant past. We might call it the missing link, for it is still missing, but must be careful not to confuse it with the missing link of popular literature—a mixture between the modern gorilla and modern man. No such form ever existed. We stem from a form that was neither human nor simian in the modern sense, and is therefore difficult to describe. Possibly *Ramapithecus* came closest to it.

On surveying the known hominid fossils, of which the oldest is a good 2,500,000 years old, we cannot help being struck by the fast evolutionary tempo of the whole group (Fig. 84). A specific human trend of evolution need not have started much before the Pliocene, 10,000,000 years ago.

It was probably the dynamism of our group which saved us from the kind of specialization to which the anthropoid apes have fallen victim. The invention of tools

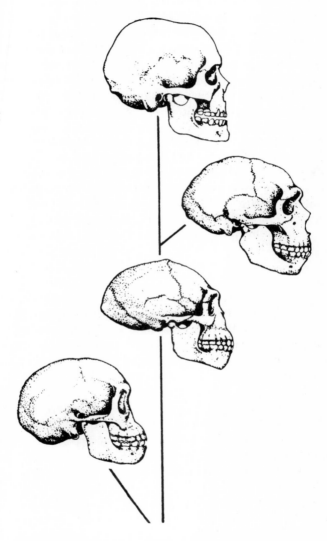

FIG. 84. Simplified family tree of man. From the bottom upwards: *Australopithecus* (of Taungs), *Sinanthropus,* modern man (Cro-Magnon); skulls. (After Romer, 1943.)

and weapons and probably also the mastery of fire changed the former tropical vegetarian into a rapacious creature that could roam throughout the world. Certain differences—between, for. instance, *Sinanthropus, Pithecanthropus,* and *Atlanthropus*—may have resulted from the breaking away of small splinter groups, which formed first a "race" and, with prolonged isolation, a special "species." This may be true of extreme Neanderthal man also. Most races, however, intermingled, and our fossils do not enable us to distinguish between what was still "race" and what had already become "species." As a result, our family tree (Fig. 73) looks like a thicket, and it seems likely that man would never have achieved his preeminent position had his evolution proceeded in a perfectly straight line.

The Development of Culture

Man cannot be conceived without his implements, nor can his history be fully described by his physical evolution alone. Hence we shall now examine the origins of man's material and intellectual culture in the light of implement and fossil finds.

Though stone was the foremost raw material of human implements, bone became important particularly toward the end of the last glacial period. Wood, too, must have played a large part, but since it is not preserved except under special conditions, we know little about it. The wooden lances from Clacton (England) and Verdun are exceptional finds.

In any case, man naturally preferred to fashion his implements from the tougher and more resistant stone. Luckily for us, stone keeps well even in strata that have lost their fossil bones by lixiviation and exposure to the weather. Since broken stone implements must be replaced, many sites hold hundreds of thousands of them. Most are, of course, only flake splinters.

The further we delve into the past, the more primitive become the tools we dig up, and we have now reached so early a stage that only an expert can tell if a given fragment is a real tool or an accidental product. The Tertiary "eoliths" (dawn stones) are no longer considered as implements; the Tertiary precursor of man does not seem to have used (recognizable) tools.

The first known stone cultures began during the Paleolithic (earliest Stone Age), when polished stone implements and pottery were unknown. That period was much longer and included many more cultures than the Mesolithic and Neolithic periods (Middle and Later Stone ages), characterized by polished axes, grave mounds, microliths, etc.

For the purposes of this book, we need only consider the earlier parts of the Paleolithic. In it there existed two main cultural trends which often overlapped. In the one, the dominant tools were heavy and thick hand axes made by chipping flint cores on both sides. In the other, the main tools were flint flakes trimmed only on one side and often with percussion bulb marks on the other. The hand ax industry was the more interesting of the two, for it represents man's successful attempt to produce a kind of universal tool for scraping, scratching, cutting, and drilling. Hand axes with striking similarities have been discovered from England in the north to the Transvaal in the south, and from Portugal in the west to India and Java in the east. They occur over most of Western Europe but are rare in Germany.

Since the various cultures were first dug up in Europe, they are known by the names of the original European sites. The dawn of hand ax cultures is represented by the Abbevillian (previously called Chellean), characterized by rough cutting edges. The next stage, the Acheulian, is distinguished by pointed or almond-shaped hand axes

FIG. 85. Late Acheulian hand axes. North Africa.
(After H. Breuil.)

(Fig. 85). Despite their French names, these cultures must have originated in Africa. In the Olduvai Gorge in Tanganyika with its successive layers, the evolution of flaked tools can be followed almost step by step. The lowest layer still contained pebbles turned into cutting instruments by the removal of one or two flakes at one end. This culture, which has no European counterpart, is known as the Oldowan. Going upward we pass, layer by layer, from a primitive Abbevillian culture to a highly developed Acheulian culture in Layer X.

As we saw, a "micro-pebble culture" was recently discovered at Vertészöllös in Hungary, a site that also yielded the remains of a human skull with Neanderthal features.

Early flake cultures include the English Clactonian in which the flakes were probably produced by striking the core on the edge of an anvil stone. The Mousterian culture of classical Neanderthal man also consisted of cut-off flakes (Fig. 86). Blades, knives, and long scrapers only appeared during the Late Paleolithic when *Homo sapiens* had begun to develop a large number of different tools.

Apart from axes, early man also produced stone missiles. Crudely finished balls were found in the Lower Pleistocene deposits of Aïn-Hanech (North Africa), and similar balls occur right up to the Acheulian of Central Africa. Leakey discovered them in groups of two to three so that he assumed that, like the South American bolas, they were strung together and used for hunting. Stone balls from Ngandong (Java), Broken Hill (Rhodesia), and La Quina (Southern France) were far more nearly perfectly rounded. Ngandong and Broken Hill had comparable stone and bone cultures.

Unfortunately, some fossil men were dug up without associated implements and cannot therefore be connected with a given stone culture. Thus Neanderthal, Mauer (Heidelberg) and Steinheim, the classic German sites, produced no proven stone tools whatsoever. A primitive flake industry is known from the upper fossil layers of Sangiran, just on top of the skull layer. Because of the scarcity of the material, we can only guess that Peking man's tools were probably of the flake type. On the other

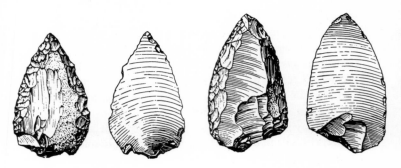

FIG. 86. Mousterian side scrapers, flaked on one side only. North Africa. (After H. Breuil.)

hand, the culture of *Atlanthropus* is associated with a primitive, and that of Swanscombe man with an advanced, hand ax industry, and so, by the way, was that of Saldanha man. Fontéchevade man is associated with a flake culture difficult to define, called the Tayacian. The Carmel culture has been discussed earlier.

Thus human culture, like mankind itself, developed by devious routes. The various cultures are typical of their age, so that many types of tool can be used as chronological pointers.

However, though tools are evidence of the degree of man's material advancement, his intellectual evolution must be inferred in more laborious and circuitous ways. To appreciate this point, we must briefly examine the history of the human individual.

Despite its relatively large body and brain, the human child is more helpless and depends far longer on its parents than the young ape. Portmann has therefore called man a prematurely born animal. Again, while large anthropoid apes reach adulthood at eleven years (Schultz), man becomes an adult at twenty.

Man's long childhood is a paramount fact of his existence. He must learn to walk, to speak, to find his way, and to become familiar with his traditions. Man could never become the social being he is without a long period of preparation.

Fossils suggest that the great dependence of the human child on its mother is an ancient trait. Thus, while orangutan remains in caves in Southern China and Sumatra contained few with milk teeth, *Australopithecus* remains and also the Choukoutien *Sinanthropus* remains contained a large number of them.

Man's evolution is inseparably linked with his ability to speak, though in Haeckel's day, people still referred to a "*Pithecanthropus alalus*" and a "*Homo stupidus*." Many students have tried to determine when man first began to speak by examining brain casts of fossil hominids for evidence of Broca's (speech) center, but all such attempts are nowadays treated with skepticism. On the other hand, legitimate inferences can be made from the structure of the lower jaw. In all apes, the inner surface of the symphysis—just behind the chin—is perfectly smooth except for the foramina introducing the nerves and the blood vessels. In man, however, the symphysis has a small triangular eminence, the mental process, to which two pairs of tongue muscles (genio-hyoid and geni-hyoglossus) are attached. Hooton has argued that the presence of the mental processes, which he called the "genial tubercles," is the surest anatomical proof of the use of articulate language. While the mental processes are not invariably ossified or detectable in early man, they are invariably absent in apes. Even if we substitute "possible use" for Hooton's overconfident assertion, it is still remarkable that the process is clearly present in *Meganthropus* (Fig. 87). The process is found in Heidelberg man, and in all

FIG. 87. Primitive lower jaw of *Meganthropus* with mental process (arrow). Natural size.

more recent human types. Though the relevant jaw fragment of *Pithecanthropus* is missing, we have good reason to assume that all the known fossil hominids were potential if not actual talkers.

Our knowledge of the magical and religious thought of fossil man bears this out. There were skeleton or head trophy cults, based on the belief that man's spiritual forces are concentrated in his brain and can be appropriated by eating the contents of the cranium. In order to get at the brain, the foramen magnum had to be widened, and many skulls from New Guinea and Borneo kept in anthropological museums show clear evidence of having received just such treatment (Fig. 88).

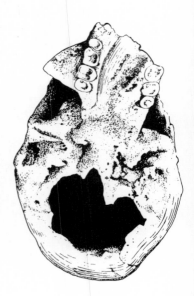

Sinanthropus   Steinheim

The Choukoutien finds tell much the same story: the remains of Peking man were smashed and scattered indiscriminately throughout the layers. All the skulls are cracked, and all their parts are known—except for the neighborhood of the foramen. Clearly the skulls were damaged systematically as were the eleven Solo skulls, and probably the Steinheim and Monte Circeo skulls.

The skull of *Pithecanthropus modjokertensis* was compressed by a violent blow from the back, and that of Ngandong V was also cracked by a blow. Krapina held the smashed remains of roughly 40 Neanderthal men.

The human remains of Taubach were deliberately damaged, and those of Fontéchevade seem to have come from

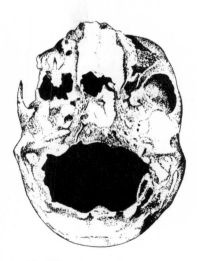 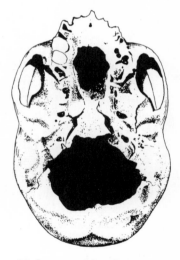

Mt. Circeo   Modern man, New Guinea

FIG. 88. Skulls with cracked bases. (After A. Blanc and F. Weidenreich.)

FIG. 89. Paleolithic "Venus stat-
uette," Willendorf, Austria.

a cannibal's kitchen midden. The Danish Mesolithic, too,
bears traces of cannibalism. In the Ofnet cave near Nörd-
lingen (Germany), 33 buried skulls were found. All had
been cut off together with the first cervical vertebra.

These examples must suffice to prove the antiquity of
cannibalism and skull hunting. The first burial sites were
associated with Neanderthal man during the last glaciation. The Le Moustier youth was buried on his side, knees
pulled up, together with his best stone implements and
probably with food for his long journey. The children's
grave at Teshik-Tash (Uzbek, U. S. S. R.) was reverently
embellished with antlers. These and other graves suggest
quite unmistakably that Neanderthal man believed in life
after death.

Neanderthal man had not yet evolved to the stage of
expressing his ideas by carvings. The first evidence of hu-

man art comes from the Aurignacian. *Homo sapiens* began his artistic career by fashioning small statues—two-dimensional representations came much later. The statues were of women, but the heads were apparently left vague, probably in order to avoid any resemblance to actual people. These figures are called "Venus statuettes." The head of the Venus of Willendorf (Fig. 89) looks like a beehive, that of Savignano resembles a fir cone, and that

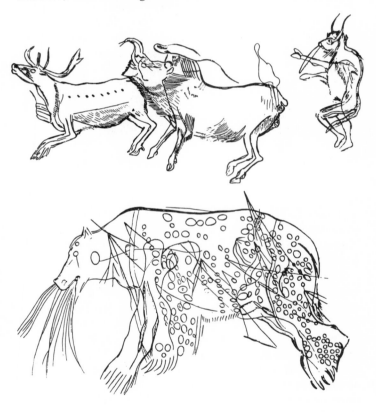

FIG. 90. Paleolithic cave paintings. Magician disguised as bison (top); magically slain cave bear (bottom). Volp Caves, Pyrenees, France. (After H. Breuil and H. Bégouen.)

of Lespugue an egg. The Venus of Brassempouy has no eyes and no mouth. Similar figures are known from all over Europe and even from Siberia. Though there is no direct evidence to this effect, the statuettes may well have been magical fertility symbols. The corpulent forms with broad hips and ample breasts probably expressed the feminine ideal of a race of undernourished hunters.

Up to the end of the Ice Age, art remained magical. On later cave paintings men invariably appeared as caricatures while such animals as mammoth, rhinoceros, horse, stag, and bison were depicted with almost unrivaled realism. Many of the animals were drawn with wounds, others are shown in or near traps, as magical attempts to influence the outcome of the hunt, or possibly to propitiate the "spirit" of the hunted animal by offering it a new abode. On some of the paintings, men are disguised as animals—mighty magicians in the midst of the herd (Fig. 90). All in all, Ice Age paintings, which are usually hidden in the most inaccessible parts of the caves, are so suffused with magic, that, admirable though they are, they cannot be called art in the modern sense.

Thus long before writing and metal were discovered, man fashioned implements, practiced head-hunting and burial rites, and painted pictures on his walls—clear signs that he did not simply take his environment for granted, but tried to mold it to his best advantage.

"Soul-bird," Lascaux caves, Southern France. (After H. Breuil.)

INDEX

Abel, 30–31, 57, 67
Adapis, 27
Aegyptopithecus Zeuxis, 30, 47, 55
Aelopithecus Chirobates, 47, 55
Africa, 17–19, 21–22, 25, 33, 43, 55–57, 98, 100, 102, 104, 109, 113, 126, 128, 144–45
Aïn-Hanech, 145
Alces latifrons, 105
Algonkian, 6, 9
Ambelodon, 18
America, 11, 15–16, 18–19, 21, 25, 27
Amphioxus, 10
Amphipithecus, 58
Ankarapithecus, 50, 55
Ankel, 57
Anthropoidea, 24–25, 27, 29, 33, 63
Anthropopithecus, 48, 55
Apidium, 63
Apidium phiomense, 63
Archaeopteryx, 2, 8
Archean, 9
Archidiskodon, 76
Arnold, Professor, 58
Asia, 17–19, 21, 25, 33, 55–58, 110
Asinus, 14
Atlanthropus, 135, 142, 146
Atlanthropus I, 100
Atlanthropus II, 100, 102
Atlanthropus III, 100
Atlanthropus mauritanicus, 100
Australanthropus, 65

Australia, 13, 41
Australopithecinae, 30, 31
Australopithecines, 65, 67–68, 72, 74–75, 77, 80, 84, 104, 126, 129
Australopithecus, 63–68, 71, 73, 74, 76, 78, 81, 82, 95, 98, 134, 141, 146
Australopithecus africanus, 63–67
Australopithecus prometheus, 63, 72
Austria, 48, 50
Austriacopithecus, 50, 55

Balanoglossus, 10
Belgium, 106
Berkheimer, 118
Bimana, 33
Black, Davidson, 91–92
Blumenbach, 33
Bohlin, Dr., 91
Bonarelli, 99
Borneo, 25, 28, 48, 85, 126, 148
Brain capacity, 38
Bramapithecus, 51, 55, 59–60
Branco, 58
Breitinger, 125
Breuil, 74
Britain, 106
Broken Hill, 109–11, 145
Broom, Dr., 63, 73, 74
Bunopithecus, 47, 55
Burma, 58

Cabot-Briggs, 102

153

Cambrian, 5–6, 8–9
Campbell, 78
Cannibalism, 93, 150
Carboniferous, 9, 14
Carmel, 123–24, 146
Catarrhina, 33
Cave paintings, 152
Ceboidea, 27–28
Cenozoic, 6, 8–9, 14, 31–32
Cercopithecinae, 62
Cercopithecines, 57, 62–63
Cercopithecoidea, 27–28, 57
Chiarelli, 57
Chimpanzee, 3, 28, 34, 43, 48, 56
China, 19, 21, 28, 46–48, 53–54, 56, 60, 85, 90–92, 96, 126, 146
Chiromys, 25
Chordates, 10
Choukoutien, 74, 91, 93, 96, 100, 146, 149
Coelodanta tichorhinus, 105
Coppens, 78
Costa Rica, 10
Cranial capacity, 130
Cretaceous, 2, 8, 14
Crista oblique, 42
Crista transversa, 40
Cro-Magnon man, 124, 141
Crossopterygii, 9, 11–12
Cuvier, 2
Cyclostomes (lampreys), 11
Cynognathus, 13
Czechoslovakia, 50, 115

Dart, Professor, 63, 72–73
Darwin, Charles, 3–4
Dawson, Charles, 127
Dental pattern, 38–41, 54, 62, 71
Dentition, 12, 42, 81–82, 135
Devonian, 9–12, 14
Diluvium, 58
Dinotherium, 18
Dryopithecinae, 30
Dryopithecus, 29, 41, 48–49, 52, 54–56, 58, 60
Dryopithecus fontani, 50, 56

"Dryopithecus pattern," 41, 62
Dubois, 85–92

East Africa, 28–29, 35, 47–48, 51, 75
Echidna, 13
Egypt, 29, 30, 45–48
Elephas, 20, 22, 76
Elephas antiquus, 105
Elephas planifrons, 19, 22
Elephas primigenius, 105
England, 25, 143
Eoanthropus, 127
Eoanthropus dawsoni, 127
Eocene, 8, 25, 27, 32, 58
Eohippus, 14–17, 21
Epimachairodus, 118
Equus, 14, 21
Equus caballus, 21
Erecta, 33
Euelephas indicus, 72
Euhomini, 66
Europe, 15–16, 18–19, 25, 28–29, 33, 48, 50, 55–57, 124, 126, 143
Eusthenopteron, 11
Eutheria, 13
Ewer, Professor, 67

Fontéchevade, 146, 149
France, 25, 46, 48, 50, 106, 121–22
Fuhlrott, J. C., 106

Geological calendar, 8, 32
Germany, 2, 4, 50, 106, 114, 143
Gibbons, 34, 56–57
Gibraltar, 116
Gieseler, 119
Giganthropus, 54, 58
Gigantopithecinae, 30
Gigantopithecus, 30, 53–55, 129–30, 140
Gigantopithecus blacki, 52
Gorilla, 28, 34, 37, 40, 54–55
Gorjanovic-Kramberger, 116
Greece, 106, 118
Greenland, 11–12

Gregory, W. K., 27, 30, 38, 41, 61–63

Haeckel, Ernest, 4, 87, 146
Heberer, 30–31, 57, 91
Hellman, 41
Henri-Martin, G., 122
Hexaprotodon, 85
Hipparion, 16, 33
Hippotigris, 14
Hispanopithecus, 47, 55
Holocene, 8, 32
Hominidae, 29–30, 33, 59–61
Hominids, 59–60, 67, 72, 74, 80, 86, 130, 136, 140
Homininae, 30
Hominine, 77, 103
Hominoid, 30, 45, 51, 52
Hominoidea, 27, 29–30, 33, 38–41, 43, 57, 63
Homo, 3, 33, 78
Homo erectus, 78, 85, 89, 98, 105
Homo habilis, 76–78
Homo heidelbergensis, 99
Homo neanderthalensis, 106, 125
Homo sapiens, 7, 34, 80, 104–5, 107, 114, 120, 124–25, 127, 129, 136–37, 145, 151
Homo troglodytes, 3
Howell, Clark, 122
Hungary, 117, 144
Hürzeler, 39, 61–62
Huxley, Thomas, 4
Hylobates, 46–47, 55, 57
Hylobatidae, 45, 47
Hylobatinae, 30
Hypocone, 40, 60
Hyracotherium, 15

Ice Age, 8, 16, 19, 21, 30, 31, 85, 106, 152
Ichthyostega, 11–12
Illiger, 33
Incus, 13
India, 19, 21–22, 29, 50, 59, 79, 143
Indo-China, 28, 48

Indopithecus, 50, 55
Italy, 106, 115

Jacob, 89
Java, 19–20, 28, 35, 47–48, 78–79, 81, 84–88, 98, 103, 113, 126, 143
Jurassic, 2, 8, 13–14

Kählin, 33
Kansupithecus, 55
Keith, 34
Kenyapithecus, 55, 60
Kleinschmidt, 115
Koenigswald, von, 78–79, 86
Kohlbrügge, 57
Kohl-Larssen, 75
Kotschke, 116
Krapina, 114, 149
Kretzoi, 118
Kromdraai, 63, 65, 66, 74

La Chapelle aux Saints, 106–8
La Chapelle man, 109, 133
La Quina, 107, 145
Latimeria, 11
Laurentian, 6
Leakey, L. S. B., 58, 60, 74, 76, 98, 145
Leakey, Mary, 70
Lewis, 56, 59–60
Limnopithecus, 35, 47, 55
Linnaeus, 3, 24, 34
Lower Eocene, 15
Lower Miocene, 28, 35, 47–48, 51–53, 55, 56, 60
Lower Oligocene, 45, 47, 55, 57, 63
Lower Pleistocene, 21, 60, 75–76, 79, 145
Lower Pliocene, 19, 21, 28, 33, 47–51, 55–57, 58–59, 63
Lower Tertiary, 14–15, 22, 25–26, 29, 62
Loxodonta africana, 76
Lungfishes (Dipnoi), 11

Madagascar, 11, 25
Makapan, 63, 72–74

Malaya, 28, 85
Malleus, 13
Marsupialia, 13
Mastodon, 21
Mastodon, 20, 22
Mastodon longirostris, 18
Mauer, 99, 121, 145
Meckel, 13
Meganthropus, 75, 79–81, 100,
    126, 130, 136, 147
Meganthropus africanus, 75
Meganthropus paleojavanicus,
    79
Mental process, 147
Mesohippus, 16
Mesolithic, 8, 143, 150
Mesozoic, 6, 8, 14
Metacone, 60
Microchoerus, 25
"Micro-pebble" culture, 118,
    144
Middle Eocene, 18
Middle Miocene, 55
Middle Pleistocene, 98
Middle Pliocene, 50, 56
Milankovitch, 31
Mindel glacial, 99
Mindel glaciation, 32, 118
Mindel-Riss interglacial, 79, 105,
    118, 120
Miocene, 8, 16, 18, 22, 32–33,
    46, 50, 56, 62, 126
Missing link, 140
Moeripithecus, 63
Moeritherium, 14, 18
Molarization, 66
"Monkey gap," 42–43, 82, 105,
    135, 137
Monotremata, 13
Montmaurin, 121–22
Mousterian, 106, 144–45

Napier, 76
Neanderthal, 105, 145
Neanderthal man, 88, 92, 102–
    10, 113–14, 117–21, 124,
    127–28, 132–34, 137–38, 142,
    144, 149–50
Necrolemur, 25

Neolithic, 8, 143
Neopilina, 10
Neopilina galatheae, 9
New Guinea, 13, 148
Ngandong, 110, 113, 145
Ngandong V, 111, 149
Ngandong VI, 111
Ngandong XI, 111–12
North America, 17
Notharctus, 27
Nycticebus, 26

Oakley, 127
Old Stone Age, 8
Olduvai, 65, 70–71, 76–78, 98,
    102, 104, 144
Oligocene, 8, 16, 25, 30, 32–33,
    43, 47, 61
Oligopithecus savagei, 47, 55
Orangutan, 34, 40, 48, 71, 86
Oreopithecoidea, 27–28
Oreopithecus, 40, 42, 61–62, 84
Oreopithecus bambolii, 62
Osborn, 61
Ostracodermi, 11

Paidopithex, 49–50, 55, 58
Pakistan, 48, 50, 60
Palaeanthropus, 99, 101
Palaeanthropus heidelbergensis,
    99
Palaeopithecus, 50, 55
Palaeosimia, 48
Paleocene, 8, 25, 32
Paleolithic, 8, 143–45, 151
Paleomastodon, 18
Paleotherium, 15
Paleozoic, 6, 9, 11
Palestine, 122–23
Paranthropus, 63, 65–66, 74, 80
Paranthropus crassidens, 65, 74
Paranthropus robustus, 65
Parapithecidae, 30, 33, 45, 57
Parapithecus, 29, 30, 45–47, 55,
    63, 83
Patterson, 78
Pei, 54, 74
Peking man, 84, 88, 92–94, 98,
    105

Perissodactyla, 66
Permian, 9, 12, 14
Peyer, 7–8
Philippines, 25
Phiomia, 18
Pilbeam, 55–56, 59
Pilgrim, 58
Piltdown man, 127–28
Pithecanthropus, 69, 72, 75–79,
    81–84, 90–92, 94, 96, 98, 100,
    102, 104–5, 124, 126–28, 134,
    137, 142, 148
Pithecanthropus I, 88, 96
Pithecanthropus II, 88–89, 96,
    113
Pithecanthropus dubius, 79, 81
Pithecanthropus erectus, 35, 78–
    79, 81, 85–90, 100–102, 131,
    137
*Pithecanthropus erectus pekin-
    ensis*, 96, 102
Pithecanthropus modjokertensis,
    35, 78–79, 81, 84, 95–96, 100,
    102, 105, 128, 135, 149
Placentalia, 13
Pleistocene, 8, 18, 21–22, 31–
    32, 35, 46–48, 53, 55, 57, 59,
    65, 75, 87, 129, 133–34
Plesianthropus, 65, 68
Plesianthropus transvaalensis, 65
Pliocene, 8, 14, 16, 19, 22, 27,
    46, 57, 76, 104, 140
Pliohippus, 16
Pliopithecus, 46–47, 50, 55, 57
Pondaugia, 58
Pongidae, 29–31, 33, 45, 58, 62,
    126
Pongids, 31, 33, 35, 43–44, 48,
    55, 57–58, 61, 63, 126, 129–30
Ponginae, 30, 61
Pongo, 48, 55
Portmann, 146
Portugal, 143
Praehomini, 65–66
Primates, 3, 33, 56
Proconsul, 35, 51, 55, 59, 140
Proconsul africanus, 53
Proconsulinae, 30, 57
Proconsul nyanzae, 52

Prohylobates, 47, 55
Propliopithecus, 29, 46–47, 55,
    63
Prosimii, 24

Quaternary, 8, 31–32

Ramapithecus, 51, 59–60, 140
Ramapithecus brevirostris, 59
Rangifer tarandus, 105
Recent (Holocene), 8, 55
Reichert, 13
Remane, 43, 83
Rhenopithecus, 50, 55
Rhinoceros etruscus, 105
Rhinoceros mercki, 105
Riss glaciation, 32
Riss and Mindel glacials, 105
Robinson, 69, 74, 77
Romer, 25
Rust, 124

Saccopastore, 115
Saldanha, 111
Sangiran, 79, 84, 87, 89, 102,
    104, 145
Sapiens, 33, 79
Schlosser, 28, 30, 45, 61–62, 91
Schoetensack, 99
Sexual dimorphism, 93, 138
Seymouria, 12
Silurian, 9, 14
Simiidae, 29, 45
Simons, 47, 55–57
Simpson, 21, 25, 29–31, 61–62,
    65
Sinanthropus, 43, 75, 88, 90,
    92–97, 100–102, 118, 126,
    128–29, 132, 135–39, 141–42,
    146, 148
Sinanthropus III, 96
Sinanthropus X, 96
Sinanthropus XI, 96
Sinanthropus pekinesis; see Pe-
    king man
Sivapithecus, 35, 48–49, 58, 60
Siwalik Hills, 35, 48–51, 57,
    59–60
Skhul, 123

Smith Woodward, Arthur, 127
Solo man, 79, 111–13, 134
South Africa, 2, 5, 11, 13, 28, 81
South America, 19, 27, 145
Soviet Union, 107, 150
Spain, 47, 50, 116
Spina mentalis, 43, 79; *see also*
    Mental process
Spy, 106
Spy I, 107
Stapes, 13
Stegodon, 19, 20–22, 111
Stegodon zdanskyi, 21
Steinheim, 118–22, 145, 148–49
Sterkfontein, 63, 65–66, 74, 98
Sugrivapithecus, 51, 55
Sumatra, 28, 47–48, 85, 126, 146
Swanscombe, 120–22, 146
Swartkrans, 63, 65–71, 74
Symphalangus, 47
Symphysis, 44, 121, 137, 147

Tarsioids, 25, 27
Tarsius, 25–26
Taungs, 63–65, 67, 74, 141
Tchadanthropus uxorius, 78
Telanthropus, 74, 98
Tertiary, 8, 31–32, 58, 60, 61,
    74, 85, 87, 127
Tertiary "eoliths," 143
Tetraprotodon, 85
Texas, 12
Theromorpha, 12
Thoma, 118

Tobias, 65, 71–72, 76–78
Torus occipitalis, 71, 118
Torus supraorbitalis, 37
Tree-shrews (Tupaioids), 25
Triassic, 8, 13
Trogontherium, 118
Tuberculum sextum, 41
Turkey, 50

Upper Devonian, 11
Upper Miocene, 55, 57, 60–61
Upper Oligocene, 55, 57
Upper Pliocene, 51, 55, 61, 104
Upper Triassic, 2, 13–14
Ursus spelaeus, 105

Vallois, 117, 121–22
Venus statuettes, 151
Vertes, 118
Villafranchian, 31–32

Wandel, 84
Weidenreich, 38, 94, 113, 115,
    128, 139
Weiner, 128
Weinert, 61, 75, 88
Woo, 97
Würm glaciation, 31–42, 105–6,
    123

Yugoslavia, 114

Zapfe, 50, 73
Zinjanthropus, 65, 69, 74, 105